Secret Bija Mantras of the Chandi Pathah

बीजमन्त्रात्मक तन्त्रदुर्गासप्तशती
गुह्यबीजनामावलि

Bījamantrātmaka Tantra Durgā Saptaśatī

Guhyabīja Nāmāvali

Translated by

स्वामी सत्यानन्द सरस्वती

Swami Satyananda Saraswati

Chaṇḍī Pāṭhaḥ, Eighth Edition
Secret Bīja Mantras of the Chaṇḍī Pāṭhaḥ
Bījamantrātmaka Guhyabījanāmāvali Tantra Durgā Saptaśatī

000721760
ISBN 978-1-877795-18-3
Library of Congress Catalog Card Number 91-075809

Cover art by Tapas Sardar

Chaṇḍī Pāṭhaḥ, Swami Satyananda Saraswati
1. Hindu Religion 2 Goddess Worship 3. Spirituality
4. Philosophy I. Saraswati, Swami Satyananda

Published by
Devi Mandir Publications
751 Mariner Loop
Yuba City, CA 95991-7532
swamiji@shreemaa.org
www.shreemaa.org

Table of Contents

Introduction

Every object in creation has two sets of names. The first is agreed upon by the customs and naming conventions of the language we are using. When we apply sounds consistently, we understand the correlation between a sound and the object to which it refers, its designated name. In Sanskrit we call this correlation the relationship between Nāma (name) and Rūpa (form).

In addition to its designated name, every object in creation has a natural name related to its intrinsic movement or vibration. Every atom contains protons, neutrons, quarks, electrons and all kinds of sub-atomic particles that are always in fluid motion. All motion creates a vibration; all vibrations create sound, whether audible to us humans or not. Those sounds are what we call the natural names of objects in creation.

In Sanskrit we call an object's natural name its Bīja, or seed, and in this way the name is inherent to the form. Nāma and Rūpa are One. The natural name is not only demonstrative, but is actually the closest audible approximation of the expression of what the object is saying itself: the name, the sound, and the vibration that it emits of its own accord.

This same phenomenon also applies to every attitude in creation, as well as to complex metaphysical concepts. Spiritual ideals such as Wisdom, Love, Peace - even Divinity and all of Creation - all have natural names. These are known as Bīja Mantras. These mantras are divine words of power that focus the mind on a desired vibration until it reaches such absorption to the exclusion of delusion.

Mantra comes from the Sanskrit words Man Trayate, that which takes away the mind. As our subjective minds lose more and more of the opinions on how we want things to be, we enter into the intuitive understanding and perception of how things actually are. We become more aligned and accepting of the reality in the here and now, and we come into the presence of understanding what is life beyond ego.

By controlling our worldly speech in thought and deed, we leave behind subjective thoughts and opinions (manas) and come into the world of objective knowledge (buddhi), in which we have no opinion. We are left only with the reality of experience; the experience of what is. We refine our thoughts from objective knowledge to mantra, refine even further from mantra to bīja, from bīja to nāda, which is the subtle body of sound, and from nāda, to Śabda Brahman, which is the sound that only God can hear.

From describing the phenomena of the external world around us, we move toward understanding the objective world within us. From mantras describing the way to unite with divinity, to natural names, which are what creation is saying of itself, to the subtle body of sound, which we can only hear within, to the divine sound that only God can hear. In this way we enter into meditation, and through practice we come to stay for longer and longer periods of time.

There are many references in various scriptures to the meaning of the bījas, and also to the meanings of each individual letter in Sanskrit. One important source is the Bīja Nighaṇṭu, which is from the Dictionaries of the Tantra Śāstra. Because these are collections of vibrations, it is difficult to ascribe specific intellectual meanings to these bījas. The vibrations will be felt by each individual in a unique way at any given time, and interpretations will vary among individuals.

It is also difficult to know whether the listener is taking in the same meaning as what the speaker is saying. Both Speaker and Listener understand in accordance with their own desires, unique experiences, and perspectives in life. Understanding is determined by so many factors: our intentions, motivations, intellectual capacity, education, association, and environment. Our Gurus will play an important role in how we apply the meanings of these bījas. Even Valmiki realized Rāma by reciting Mara Mara, which means: dead body, dead body, the name of Rāma backwards.

The Pāṇini Sanskrit grammar defines the meanings of each of the letters. We call the letters Mātṛkās, or Divine Mothers. These Divine Mothers give birth to the forms of expression of each vibration, each letter. The combinations of the letters create the bījas, which are the natural names realized in meditation by the Ṛṣis, the Seers of Divine Truth.

The Ṛṣis were inspired poets longing for divinity; beings of wisdom and harmony who wrote their inspirations of clarity, unity, universal love and acceptance. When we recite scripture, we want to maintain the same intentions and motivations as the Ṛṣis had, giving up our selfishness so we can intuitively recognize

Vasudhaiva Kuṭumbakam, the whole world is one Family. If all of creation is one Family, then it stands to reason that there is one Mother and one Father to whom we all owe allegiance. We call that Mother and Father figure God, who has many names by which we can choose to call: the Supreme Divinity, Oṃ, the Infinite Beyond Conception, Śiva, Śakti, or Chaṇḍī for example. The purpose for our performing sādhana is to come into harmony with that realization of God, that Divinity, in every thought and action we perform.

Traditionally all ancient knowledge was divided into Śruti and Smṛti, that which was transmitted verbally from Guru to disciple is the oral tradition, and that which was written down using various materials, and studied or recited formed scripture. The Chaṇḍī Pāṭhaḥ came from Mārkaṇḍeya Purāṇa, which dates somewhere between 900 BCE and 500 BCE, although it was not written down until around 300 BCE.

The entire Chaṇḍī Pāṭhaḥ purports to be a bridge or commentary on the two Rig Vedic hymns included at its beginning and end: the Rātri Sūktam, Praise to the Night of Duality, and the Devi Sūktam, Praise to the Goddess who is Unity. The 700 verses of Durgā Saptaśatī, or Chaṇḍī Pāṭhaḥ, tell us how to make the journey from duality to unity, by calling upon the Divine Mother to withdraw Her energy from negativity and give it unequivocally to positivity.

Those two hymns are from the oldest portions of Ṛg Veda, so they may date somewhere between 2,000 and 5,000 BCE, and according to Wikipedia, between 4,000 and 12,000 BCE, although nobody knows for sure. Obviously, this was part of Śruti, the portion that was transmitted orally, as likely were the bīja mantras connected with each chapter.

It appears that in 300 BCE when the Chaṇḍī Pāṭhaḥ was written down, the more esoteric teachings containing the bīja mantras were not recorded in writing. We do not know when this changed, as there is no scriptural reference to these mantras. It is probably part of the oral tradition.

It is possible that an ancient manuscript of the text exists in the Nepal National Library, but presently we cannot verify that claim. What is verifiable is that this Bījamantrātmaka Saptaśatī is a work of such significant importance that sadhus are still using it today.

The oldest publication of these mantras I have seen was from 1900, but that appears to be a mistake in the cataloging data. My collection contains a version that was published in 1973, and another version printed in 1998. Whatever the exact history, it is certainly not a product of modern contrivance.

While the text does not appear in any scripture because of the nature of its oral transmission, it has sufficient bhāvana that we should not spend too much energy debating its authenticity, lineage, or history, but rather study how we can use it to complement and enhance the disciplines and recitations we are already performing.

Once we have defined our intention to live the life of a Ṛṣi, and we are motivated to pursue the highest ideal in every definition we contemplate, it behooves us to seek the greatest spiritual wealth from every syllable we utter. If we take the highest meaning of every letter which is constituent in the bīja, we can raise our understanding of what the Ṛṣis actually felt when they were reciting these texts.

There are three ways in which we can use these mantras. We can intersperse the mantras as samputṣ to the seven hundred verses in accordance with the traditions of our lineage. Some may choose to recite only the bīja mantras, and others may unite the bīja mantras with the verses of Durgā Saptaśatī. According to these three methods, sadhus can choose to perform japa, recitation, homa, or other types of sādhana.

No matter what way we choose, and it can vary from sankalpa to sankalpa according to the definition of the worshiper, reciting the bījas, the natural names, of all the verses of the Chaṇḍī Pāṭhaḥ, and contemplating the meanings of the bījas and the verses, will generate added enhancement to the bhāvana, to the feeling, to intuitive cognition, and to the intensity of our reality, and will bring more of these vibrations into sharper focus.

The bīja mantras were researched from Śrī Tantra Durgā Saptaśatī by Shivadattashashtri published in 1973 in Kanpur.

The Tantrik Chaṇḍī Paddhoti showing the use of the bīja mantras in the Saptaśatī text uses the Saptaśatya Guhyabījanāmāvali by Dr. Ramchandra Puri, published by Chaukhamba in Dehli in 1998. The cover art was provided by Tapas Sardar.

With the blessings of Shree Maa, I want to thank Ekatma, Shivani, Adaitya, Rani, Papia, Pushpa, and all of the Devi Mandir Family for all of their contributions in bringing this effort to fruition.

Swami Satyananda, 2019

आदिशक्तये नमः

श्रीतन्त्रदुर्गासप्तशती

विश्वेश्वरीं विश्वमयीं
विरूपामज्ञानहन्त्रीं विमलस्वरूपाम् ।
शश्वत्प्रसन्नाङ्करुणावतारान्
तन्त्रस्वरूपाञ्चनमामिदुर्गाम् ॥ १ ॥

चिदानन्दरूपे हरीशादिवन्द्ये
सदामन्दहासे जगद्भीतिनाशे ।
चिदानन्ददेत्वञ्च तन्त्रस्वरूपेजनं
पाहिदीनन्तवार्चाविहीनम् ॥ २ ॥

नजानातिविष्णुःशिवोनैववेत्तिस्वयम्भूः
स्वयन्नैवजानातिमातः ।
चरित्रन्दयाधारिके ते विचित्रङ्कथन्मन्द
बुद्धिर्जनःस्यात्समर्थ ॥ ३ ॥

तथाप्यम्बलोलोपकारायलोकेचरित्रं
वदाम्यत्रकिञ्चित्प्रसिद्धम् ।
तवप्रेरणैवाभवद्हेतुभूतामदीयेहृदब्जे
महादेविदुर्गे ॥ ४ ॥

तन्त्ररूपं रात्रिसूक्तम्

1. ॐ ऐं ब्लूं नमः
2. ॐ ऐं ठां नमः
3. ॐ ऐं ह्रीं नमः
4. ॐ ऐं स्त्रां नमः
5. ॐ ऐं स्लूं नमः
6. ॐ ऐं क्रैं नमः
7. ॐ ऐं त्रां नमः
8. ॐ ऐं फ्रां नमः
9. ॐ ऐं जीं नमः
10. ॐ ऐं लूं नमः
11. ॐ ऐं स्लूं नमः
12. ॐ ऐं नों नमः
13. ॐ ऐं स्त्रीं नमः

14. ॐ ऐं प्रूं नमः

15. ॐ ऐं स्त्रूं नमः

16. ॐ ऐं जां नमः

17. ॐ ऐं वौं नमः

18. ॐ ऐं ओं नमः

इति तन्त्ररूपं रात्रिसूक्तम्

ॐ ऐं ह्रीं क्लीं चामुण्डायै विच्चे
ॐ बीजत्रयायैविद्महे तत्प्रधानायैधीमहि
तन्नः शक्तिः प्राचोदयात्

अथ प्रथमोऽध्यायः

1. ॐ ऐं श्रीं नमः
2. ॐ ऐं ह्रीं नमः
3. ॐ ऐं क्लीं नमः
4. ॐ ऐं श्रीं नमः
5. ॐ ऐं प्रीं नमः
6. ॐ ऐं ह्रां नमः
7. ॐ ऐं ह्रीं नमः
8. ॐ ऐं सौं नमः
9. ॐ ऐं प्रें नमः
10. ॐ ऐं म्रीं नमः
11. ॐ ऐं ह्लीं नमः
12. ॐ ऐं म्लीं नमः
13. ॐ ऐं स्त्रीं नमः

14. ॐ ऐं क्रां नमः

15. ॐ ऐं ह्स्लीं नमः

16. ॐ ऐं क्रीं नमः

17. ॐ ऐं चां नमः

18. ॐ ऐं में नमः

19. ॐ ऐं क्रीं नमः

20. ॐ ऐं वैं नमः

21. ॐ ऐं ह्रौं नमः

22. ॐ ऐं युं नमः

23. ॐ ऐं जुं नमः

24. ॐ ऐं हं नमः

25. ॐ ऐं शं नमः

26. ॐ ऐं रौं नमः

27. ॐ ऐं यं नमः

28. ॐ ऐं विं नमः

29. ॐ ऐं वैं नमः

30. ॐ ऐं चें नमः

31. ॐ ऐं ह्रीं नमः

32. ॐ ऐं क्रं नमः

33. ॐ ऐं सं नमः

34. ॐ ऐं कं नमः

35. ॐ ऐं श्रीं नमः

36. ॐ ऐं त्रौं नमः

37. ॐ ऐं स्त्रां नमः

38. ॐ ऐं ज्यैं नमः

39. ॐ ऐं रौं नमः

40. ॐ ऐं द्रां नमः

41. ॐ ऐं द्रों नमः

42. ॐ ऐं ह्रां नमः

43. ॐ ऐं द्रूं नमः

44. ॐ ऐं शां नमः

45. ॐ ऐं मीं नमः

46. ॐ ऐं श्रौं नमः

47. ॐ ऐं जुं नमः

48. ॐ ऐं ह्लूं नमः

49. ॐ ऐं श्रूं नमः

50. ॐ ऐं प्रीं नमः

51. ॐ ऐं रं नमः

52. ॐ ऐं वं नमः

53. ॐ ऐं ब्रीं नमः

54. ॐ ऐं ब्लं नमः

55. ॐ ऐं स्रौं नमः

56. ॐ ऐं ल्वां नमः

57. ॐ ऐं लूं नमः

58. ॐ ऐं सां नमः

59. ॐ ऐं रौं नमः

60. ॐ ऐं स्हौं नमः

61. ॐ ऐं कुं नमः

62. ॐ ऐं शौं नमः

63. ॐ ऐं श्रौं नमः

64. ॐ ऐं वं नमः

65. ॐ ऐं त्रूं नमः

66. ॐ ऐं क्रौं नमः

67. ॐ ऐं क्लुं नमः

68. ॐ ऐं क्लीं नमः

69. ॐ ऐं श्रीं नमः

70. ॐ ऐं ब्लूं नमः

71. ॐ ऐं ठां नमः

72. ॐ ऐं ह्रीं नमः

73. ॐ ऐं स्त्रां नमः

74. ॐ ऐं स्ल्रूं नमः

75. ॐ ऐं क्रैं नमः

76. ॐ ऐं त्रां नमः

77. ॐ ऐं फ्रां नमः

78. ॐ ऐं जीं नमः

79. ॐ ऐं लूं नमः

80. ॐ ऐं स्ल्रूं नमः

81. ॐ ऐं नों नमः

82. ॐ ऐं स्त्रीं नमः

83. ॐ ऐं प्रूं नमः

84. ॐ ऐं सूं नमः

85. ॐ ऐं ज्रां नमः

86. ॐ ऐं वौं नमः

87. ॐ ऐं ओं नमः

88. ॐ ऐं श्रौं नमः

89. ॐ ऐं त्रृं नमः

90. ॐ ऐं रूं नमः

91. ॐ ऐं क्लीं नमः

92. ॐ ऐं दुं नमः

93. ॐ ऐं ह्रीं नमः

94. ॐ ऐं गूं नमः

95. ॐ ऐं लां नमः

96. ॐ ऐं ह्रां नमः

97. ॐ ऐं गं नमः

98. ॐ ऐं ऐं नमः

99. ॐ ऐं श्रौं नमः

100. ॐ ऐं जूं नमः

101. ॐ ऐं डें नमः

102. ॐ ऐं श्रौं नमः

103. ॐ ऐं छां नमः

104. ॐ ऐं क्लीं नमः

ॐ श्रीं क्लीं ह्लीं ह्लीं फट् स्वाहा

इति प्रथमोऽध्यायः

अथ द्वितीयोऽध्यायः

1. ॐ ऐं श्रौं नमः
2. ॐ ऐं श्रीं नमः
3. ॐ ऐं ह्सूं नमः
4. ॐ ऐं हौं नमः
5. ॐ ऐं ह्रीं नमः
6. ॐ ऐं अं नमः
7. ॐ ऐं क्लीं नमः
8. ॐ ऐं चां नमः
9. ॐ ऐं मुं नमः
10. ॐ ऐं डां नमः
11. ॐ ऐं यैं नमः
12. ॐ ऐं विं नमः
13. ॐ ऐं च्चें नमः

14. ॐ ऐं ईं नमः

15. ॐ ऐं सौं नमः

16. ॐ ऐं व्रां नमः

17. ॐ ऐं त्रौं नमः

18. ॐ ऐं लूं नमः

19. ॐ ऐं वं नमः

20. ॐ ऐं ह्रां नमः

21. ॐ ऐं क्रीं नमः

22. ॐ ऐं सौं नमः

23. ॐ ऐं यं नमः

24. ॐ ऐं ऐं नमः

25. ॐ ऐं मूं नमः

26. ॐ ऐं सः नमः

27. ॐ ऐं हं नमः

28. ॐ ऐं सं नमः

29. ॐ ऐं सों नमः

30. ॐ ऐं शं नमः

31. ॐ ऐं हं नमः

32. ॐ ऐं ह्लौं नमः

33. ॐ ऐं ह्लीं नमः

34. ॐ ऐं यूं नमः

35. ॐ ऐं त्रूं नमः

36. ॐ ऐं स्त्रीं नमः

37. ॐ ऐं आं नमः

38. ॐ ऐं प्रें नमः

39. ॐ ऐं शं नमः

40. ॐ ऐं ह्लां नमः

41. ॐ ऐं स्मूं नमः

42. ॐ ऐं ऊं नमः

43. ॐ ऐं गूं नमः

44. ॐ ऐं व्यं नमः

45. ॐ ऐं ह्लं नमः

46. ॐ ऐं भैं नमः

47. ॐ ऐं ह्लां नमः

48. ॐ ऐं क्रूं नमः

49. ॐ ऐं मूं नमः

50. ॐ ऐं ल्रीं नमः

51. ॐ ऐं श्रां नमः

52. ॐ ऐं द्रूं नमः

53. ॐ ऐं ह्लूं नमः

54. ॐ ऐं ह्सौं नमः

55. ॐ ऐं क्रां नमः

56. ॐ ऐं स्हौं नमः

57. ॐ ऐं म्लूं नमः

58. ॐ ऐं श्रीं नमः

59. ॐ ऐं गैं नमः

60. ॐ ऐं क्रीं नमः

61. ॐ ऐं त्रीं नमः

62. ॐ ऐं क्सीं नमः

63. ॐ ऐं फ्रों नमः

64. ॐ ऐं फ्रैं नमः

65. ॐ ऐं ह्रीं नमः

66. ॐ ऐं शां नमः

67. ॐ ऐं क्ष्म्रीं नमः

68. ॐ ऐं रौं नमः

69. ॐ ऐं ड्रूं नमः

ॐ ऐं क्रीं क्रां सौं सः फट् स्वाहा

इति द्वितीयोऽध्यायः

अथ तृतीयोऽध्यायः

1. ॐ ऐं श्रौं नमः
2. ॐ ऐं क्लीं नमः
3. ॐ ऐं सां नमः
4. ॐ ऐं त्रों नमः
5. ॐ ऐं प्रूं नमः
6. ॐ ऐं ग्लौं नमः
7. ॐ ऐं क्रौं नमः
8. ॐ ऐं व्रीं नमः
9. ॐ ऐं स्लीं नमः
10. ॐ ऐं ह्लीं नमः
11. ॐ ऐं हौं नमः
12. ॐ ऐं श्रां नमः
13. ॐ ऐं ग्रीं नमः

14. ॐ ऐं क्रूं नमः

15. ॐ ऐं क्रीं नमः

16. ॐ ऐं यां नमः

17. ॐ ऐं द्लूं नमः

18. ॐ ऐं द्रूं नमः

19. ॐ ऐं क्षं नमः

20. ॐ ऐं ओं नमः

21. ॐ ऐं क्रौं नमः

22. ॐ ऐं क्ष्म्क्लरीं नमः

23. ॐ ऐं वां नमः

24. ॐ ऐं श्रूं नमः

25. ॐ ऐं ग्लूं नमः

26. ॐ ऐं ल्रीं नमः

27. ॐ ऐं प्रें नमः

28. ॐ ऐं हूं नमः

29. ॐ ऐं ह्रौं नमः

30. ॐ ऐं दें नमः

31. ॐ ऐं नूं नमः

32. ॐ ऐं आं नमः

33. ॐ ऐं फ्रां नमः

34. ॐ ऐं प्रीं नमः

35. ॐ ऐं दं नमः

36. ॐ ऐं फ्रीं नमः

37. ॐ ऐं ह्रीं नमः

38. ॐ ऐं गूं नमः

39. ॐ ऐं श्रौं नमः

40. ॐ ऐं सां नमः

41. ॐ ऐं श्रीं नमः

42. ॐ ऐं जुं नमः

43. ॐ ऐं हं नमः

44. ॐ ऐं सं नमः

ॐ ह्रीं श्रीं कुं फट् स्वाहा

इति तृतीयोऽध्यायः

अथ चतुर्थोऽध्यायः

1. ॐ ऐं श्रौं नमः
2. ॐ ऐं सौं नमः
3. ॐ ऐं दीं नमः
4. ॐ ऐं प्रें नमः
5. ॐ ऐं यां नमः
6. ॐ ऐं रूं नमः
7. ॐ ऐं मं नमः
8. ॐ ऐं सूं नमः
9. ॐ ऐं श्रां नमः
10. ॐ ऐं औं नमः
11. ॐ ऐं लूं नमः
12. ॐ ऐं डूं नमः
13. ॐ ऐं जूं नमः

14. ॐ ऐं धूं नमः

15. ॐ ऐं त्रें नमः

16. ॐ ऐं ह्रीं नमः

17. ॐ ऐं श्रीं नमः

18. ॐ ऐं ईं नमः

19. ॐ ऐं ह्रां नमः

20. ॐ ऐं ह्ल्रूं नमः

21. ॐ ऐं क्लूं नमः

22. ॐ ऐं क्रां नमः

23. ॐ ऐं ह्लूं नमः

24. ॐ ऐं फ्रें नमः

25. ॐ ऐं क्रीं नमः

26. ॐ ऐं स्लूं नमः

27. ॐ ऐं घ्रें नमः

28. ॐ ऐं श्रौं नमः

29. ॐ ऐं ह्रौं नमः

30. ॐ ऐं व्रीं नमः

31. ॐ ऐं ह्रीं नमः

32. ॐ ऐं त्रौं नमः

33. ॐ ऐं ह्लौं नमः

34. ॐ ऐं गीं नमः

35. ॐ ऐं यूं नमः

36. ॐ ऐं ह्लीं नमः

37. ॐ ऐं ह्लूं नमः

38. ॐ ऐं श्रौं नमः

39. ॐ ऐं ओं नमः

40. ॐ ऐं अं नमः

41. ॐ ऐं म्हौं नमः

42. ॐ ऐं प्रीं नमः

ॐ अं ह्लीं श्रीं हंसः फट् स्वाहा

इति चतुर्थोऽध्यायः

अथ पञ्चमोऽध्यायः

1. ॐ ऐं श्रौं नमः
2. ॐ ऐं प्रीं नमः
3. ॐ ऐं ओं नमः
4. ॐ ऐं ह्रीं नमः
5. ॐ ऐं ल्रीं नमः
6. ॐ ऐं त्रों नमः
7. ॐ ऐं क्रीं नमः
8. ॐ ऐं ह्सौं नमः
9. ॐ ऐं ह्रीं नमः
10. ॐ ऐं श्रीं नमः
11. ॐ ऐं हूं नमः
12. ॐ ऐं क्लीं नमः
13. ॐ ऐं रौं नमः

14. ॐ ऐं स्त्रीं नमः

15. ॐ ऐं ह्लीं नमः

16. ॐ ऐं प्लूं नमः

17. ॐ ऐं स्हौं नमः

18. ॐ ऐं स्त्रीं नमः

19. ॐ ऐं ग्लूं नमः

20. ॐ ऐं व्रीं नमः

21. ॐ ऐं सौं नमः

22. ॐ ऐं लूं नमः

23. ॐ ऐं ह्लूं नमः

24. ॐ ऐं द्रां नमः

25. ॐ ऐं क्सां नमः

26. ॐ ऐं क्ष्म्रीं नमः

27. ॐ ऐं ग्लौं नमः

28. ॐ ऐं स्कं नमः

29. ॐ ऐं बूं नमः

30. ॐ ऐं स्क्लूं नमः

31. ॐ ऐं क्रौं नमः

32. ॐ ऐं छ्रीं नमः

33. ॐ ऐं स्लूं नमः

34. ॐ ऐं क्लूं नमः

35. ॐ ऐं शां नमः

36. ॐ ऐं ल्हीं नमः

37. ॐ ऐं स्त्रूं नमः

38. ॐ ऐं ह्लीं नमः

39. ॐ ऐं लीं नमः

40. ॐ ऐं सं नमः

41. ॐ ऐं लूं नमः

42. ॐ ऐं ह्सूं नमः

43. ॐ ऐं श्रूं नमः

44. ॐ ऐं जूं नमः

45. ॐ ऐं ह्स्ल्रीं नमः

46. ॐ ऐं स्कीं नमः

47. ॐ ऐं क्लां नमः

48. ॐ ऐं श्रूं नमः

49. ॐ ऐं हं नमः

50. ॐ ऐं ह्लीं नमः

51. ॐ ऐं क्स्त्रूं नमः

52. ॐ ऐं द्रौं नमः

53. ॐ ऐं क्लूं नमः

54. ॐ ऐं गां नमः

55. ॐ ऐं सं नमः

56. ॐ ऐं ल्स्त्रां नमः

57. ॐ ऐं फ्रीं नमः

58. ॐ ऐं स्लां नमः

59. ॐ ऐं ल्लूं नमः

60. ॐ ऐं फ्रें नमः

61. ॐ ऐं ओं नमः

62. ॐ ऐं स्ह्लीं नमः

63. ॐ ऐं ह्लां नमः

64. ॐ ऐं ॐ नमः

65. ॐ ऐं ह्लूं नमः

66. ॐ ऐं हूँ नमः

67. ॐ ऐं नं नमः

68. ॐ ऐं स्त्रां नमः

69. ॐ ऐं वं नमः

70. ॐ ऐं मं नमः

71. ॐ ऐं म्ब्लीं नमः

72. ॐ ऐं शां नमः

73. ॐ ऐं लं नमः

74. ॐ ऐं भैं नमः

75. ॐ ऐं ह्लूं नमः

76. ॐ ऐं हौं नमः

77. ॐ ऐं ईं नमः

78. ॐ ऐं चें नमः

79. ॐ ऐं ल्क्रीं नमः

80. ॐ ऐं ह्लीं नमः

81. ॐ ऐं क्ष्म्ल्रीं नमः

82. ॐ ऐं पूं नमः

83. ॐ ऐं श्रौं नमः

84. ॐ ऐं ह्रौं नमः

85. ॐ ऐं भ्रूं नमः

86. ॐ ऐं क्स्त्रीं नमः

87. ॐ ऐं आं नमः

88. ॐ ऐं क्रूं नमः

89. ॐ ऐं त्रूं नमः

90. ॐ ऐं ड्रुं नमः

91. ॐ ऐं जां नमः

92. ॐ ऐं ह्लूं नमः

93. ॐ ऐं फ्रौं नमः

94. ॐ ऐं क्रौं नमः

95. ॐ ऐं किं नमः

96. ॐ ऐं ग्लूं नमः

97. ॐ ऐं छ्र्क्लीं नमः

98. ॐ ऐं रं नमः

99. ॐ ऐं क्सैं नमः

100. ॐ ऐं स्हुं नमः

101. ॐ ऐं श्रौं नमः

102. ॐ ऐं श्श्रीं नमः

103. ॐ ऐं ओं नमः

104. ॐ ऐं ल्ूं नमः

105. ॐ ऐं ल्हूं नमः

106. ॐ ऐं ह्लूं नमः

107. ॐ ऐं स्क्रीं नमः

108. ॐ ऐं स्त्रौं नमः

109. ॐ ऐं स्भ्रूं नमः

110. ॐ ऐं क्ष्म्क्लीं नमः

111. ॐ ऐं व्रीं नमः

112. ॐ ऐं सीं नमः

113. ॐ ऐं भूं नमः

114. ॐ ऐं लां नमः

115. ॐ ऐं श्रौं नमः

116. ॐ ऐं स्हैं नमः

117. ॐ ऐं ह्रीं नमः

118. ॐ ऐं श्रीं नमः

119. ॐ ऐं फ्रें नमः

120. ॐ ऐं स्लूंनमः

121. ॐ ऐं च्छ्रूं नमः

122. ॐ ऐं ल्हूं नमः

123. ॐ ऐं कंनमः

124. ॐ ऐं द्रें नमः

125. ॐ ऐं श्रीं नमः

126. ॐ ऐं सां नमः

127. ॐ ऐं ह्रीं नमः

128. ॐ ऐं ऐं नमः

129. ॐ ऐं स्क्लीं नमः

ओं ऐं ह्रीं क्लीं चामुण्डायै विच्चे स्वाहा

इति पञ्चमोऽध्यायः

अथ षष्ठोऽध्यायः

1. ॐ ऐं श्रौं नमः
2. ॐ ऐं ओं नमः
3. ॐ ऐं त्रूं नमः
4. ॐ ऐं ह्रौं नमः
5. ॐ ऐं क्रौं नमः
6. ॐ ऐं ह्रीं नमः
7. ॐ ऐं त्रीं नमः
8. ॐ ऐं क्लीं नमः
9. ॐ ऐं प्रीं नमः
10. ॐ ऐं ह्रीं नमः
11. ॐ ऐं ह्रौं नमः
12. ॐ ऐं श्रौं नमः
13. ॐ ऐं ऐं नमः

14. ॐ ऐं ओं नमः

15. ॐ ऐं श्रीं नमः

16. ॐ ऐं क्रां नमः

17. ॐ ऐं हूं नमः

18. ॐ ऐं छ्रां नमः

19. ॐ ऐं क्ष्म्क्ल्रीं नमः

20. ॐ ऐं ह्लूं नमः

21. ॐ ऐं सौं नमः

22. ॐ ऐं ह्लौं नमः

23. ॐ ऐं क्रूं नमः

24. ॐ ऐं सौं नमः

ॐ श्रीं यं ह्रीं क्लीं ह्रीं फट् स्वाहा

इति षष्ठोऽध्यायः

अथ सप्तमोऽध्यायः

1. ॐ ऐं श्रौं नमः
2. ॐ ऐं कूं नमः
3. ॐ ऐं ह्लीं नमः
4. ॐ ऐं ह्लं नमः
5. ॐ ऐं मूं नमः
6. ॐ ऐं त्रौं नमः
7. ॐ ऐं ह्लौं नमः
8. ॐ ऐं ओं नमः
9. ॐ ऐं ह्सूं नमः
10. ॐ ऐं क्लूं नमः
11. ॐ ऐं क्रें नमः
12. ॐ ऐं नें नमः
13. ॐ ऐं लूं नमः

14. ॐ ऐं ह्स्लीं नमः

15. ॐ ऐं प्लूं नमः

16. ॐ ऐं शां नमः

17. ॐ ऐं स्लूं नमः

18. ॐ ऐं प्लीं नमः

19. ॐ ऐं प्रें नमः

20. ॐ ऐं अं नमः

21. ॐ ऐं औं नमः

22. ॐ ऐं म्ल्रीं नमः

23. ॐ ऐं श्रां नमः

24. ॐ ऐं सौं नमः

25. ॐ ऐं श्रौं नमः

26. ॐ ऐं प्रीं नमः

27. ॐ ऐं ह्स्व्रीं नमः

ॐ रं रं रं कं कं कं जं जं जं

चामुण्डायै फट् स्वाहा

इति सप्तमोध्यायः

अथाष्टमोऽध्यायः

1. ॐ ऐं श्रौं नमः
2. ॐ ऐं म्ह्लीं नमः
3. ॐ ऐं प्रूं नमः
4. ॐ ऐं ऐं नमः
5. ॐ ऐं क्रों नमः
6. ॐ ऐं ईं नमः
7. ॐ ऐं ऐं नमः
8. ॐ ऐं ल्रीं नमः
9. ॐ ऐं फ्रौं नमः
10. ॐ ऐं म्लूं नमः
11. ॐ ऐं नों नमः
12. ॐ ऐं हूं नमः
13. ॐ ऐं फ्रौं नमः

14. ॐ ऐं ग्लौं नमः

15. ॐ ऐं स्मौं नमः

16. ॐ ऐं सौं नमः

17. ॐ ऐं श्रीं नमः

18. ॐ ऐं स्हौं नमः

19. ॐ ऐं ख्सें नमः

20. ॐ ऐं क्ष्म्लीं नमः

21. ॐ ऐं ह्रां नमः

22. ॐ ऐं वीं नमः

23. ॐ ऐं लूं नमः

24. ॐ ऐं ल्सीं नमः

25. ॐ ऐं ब्लीं नमः

26. ॐ ऐं त्स्रों नमः

27. ॐ ऐं व्रूं नमः

28. ॐ ऐं श्ल्कीं नमः

29. ॐ ऐं श्रूं नमः

30. ॐ ऐं ह्रीं नमः

31. ॐ ऐं शीं नमः

32. ॐ ऐं क्लीं नमः

33. ॐ ऐं क्लौं नमः

34. ॐ ऐं तीं नमः

35. ॐ ऐं ह्रूं नमः

36. ॐ ऐं क्लूं नमः

37. ॐ ऐं तां नमः

38. ॐ ऐं ह्लूं नमः

39. ॐ ऐं हं नमः

40. ॐ ऐं स्लूं नमः

41. ॐ ऐं औं नमः

42. ॐ ऐं ल्हौं नमः

43. ॐ ऐं श्लीं नमः

44. ॐ ऐं यां नमः

45. ॐ ऐं थ्लीं नमः

46. ॐ ऐं ल्हों नमः

47. ॐ ऐं ग्लौं नमः

48. ॐ ऐं ह्रौं नमः

49. ॐ ऐं प्रां नमः

50. ॐ ऐं क्रीं नमः

51. ॐ ऐं क्लीं नमः

52. ॐ ऐं न्स्लुं नमः

53. ॐ ऐं हीं नमः

54. ॐ ऐं ह्लौं नमः

55. ॐ ऐं ह्रैं नमः

56. ॐ ऐं भ्रं नमः

57. ॐ ऐं सौं नमः

58. ॐ ऐं श्रीं नमः

59. ॐ ऐं प्सूं नमः

60. ॐ ऐं द्रौं नमः

61. ॐ ऐं स्त्रां नमः

62. ॐ ऐं ह्स्लीं नमः

63. ॐ ऐं स्ल्ल्रीं नमः

ॐ शां सं श्रीं श्रं अं अः क्लीं हीं फट् स्वाहा

इत्यष्टमोऽध्यायः

अथ नवमोऽध्यायः

1. ॐ ऐं रौं नमः
2. ॐ ऐं क्लीं नमः
3. ॐ ऐं म्लौं नमः
4. ॐ ऐं श्रौं नमः
5. ॐ ऐं ग्लीं नमः
6. ॐ ऐं ह्रौं नमः
7. ॐ ऐं ह्सौं नमः
8. ॐ ऐं ईं नमः
9. ॐ ऐं ब्रूं नमः
10. ॐ ऐं श्रां नमः
11. ॐ ऐं लूं नमः
12. ॐ ऐं आं नमः
13. ॐ ऐं श्रीं नमः

14. ॐ ऐं क्रौं नमः

15. ॐ ऐं प्रूं नमः

16. ॐ ऐं क्लीं नमः

17. ॐ ऐं भ्रूं नमः

18. ॐ ऐं ह्लौं नमः

19. ॐ ऐं क्रीं नमः

20. ॐ ऐं म्लीं नमः

21. ॐ ऐं ग्लौं नमः

22. ॐ ऐं ह्सूं नमः

23. ॐ ऐं ल्पीं नमः

24. ॐ ऐं ह्लौं नमः

25. ॐ ऐं ह्स्त्रां नमः

26. ॐ ऐं स्हौं नमः

27. ॐ ऐं ह्लूं नमः

28. ॐ ऐं क्स्लीं नमः

29. ॐ ऐं श्रीं नमः

30. ॐ ऐं स्तूं नमः

31. ॐ ऐं च्रें नमः

32. ॐ ऐं वीं नमः

33. ॐ ऐं क्ष्लूं नमः

34. ॐ ऐं श्लूं नमः

35. ॐ ऐं क्रूं नमः

36. ॐ ऐं क्रां नमः

37. ॐ ऐं ह्रौं नमः

38. ॐ ऐं क्रां नमः

39. ॐ ऐं स्क्ष्लीं नमः

40. ॐ ऐं सूं नमः

41. ॐ ऐं फ्रूं नमः

ॐ ऐं ह्रीं श्रीं सौं फट् स्वाहा

इति नवमोऽध्यायः

अथ दशमोऽध्यायः

1. ॐ ऐं श्रौं नमः
2. ॐ ऐं ह्रीं नमः
3. ॐ ऐं ब्लूं नमः
4. ॐ ऐं ह्रीं नमः
5. ॐ ऐं म्लूं नमः
6. ॐ ऐं श्रौं नमः
7. ॐ ऐं ह्रीं नमः
8. ॐ ऐं ग्लीं नमः
9. ॐ ऐं श्रौं नमः
10. ॐ ऐं ध्रूं नमः
11. ॐ ऐं हुं नमः
12. ॐ ऐं द्रौं नमः
13. ॐ ऐं श्रीं नमः

14. ॐ ऐं त्रूं नमः

15. ॐ ऐं व्रूं नमः

16. ॐ ऐं फ्रें नमः

17. ॐ ऐं ह्वां नमः

18. ॐ ऐं जुं नमः

19. ॐ ऐं स्त्रौं नमः

20. ॐ ऐं स्लूं नमः

21. ॐ ऐं प्रें नमः

22. ॐ ऐं ह्स्वां नमः

23. ॐ ऐं प्रीं नमः

24. ॐ ऐं फ्रां नमः

25. ॐ ऐं क्रीं नमः

26. ॐ ऐं श्रीं नमः

27. ॐ ऐं क्रां नमः

28. ॐ ऐं सः नमः

29. ॐ ऐं क्लीं नमः

30. ॐ ऐं व्रें नमः

31. ॐ ऐं ईं नमः

32. ॐ ऐं ज्स्ह्ल्रीं नमः

ॐ ऐं ह्रीं नमः क्लीं ह्रीं फट् स्वाहा

इति दशमोऽध्यायः

अथ एकादशोऽध्यायः

1. ॐ ऐं श्रौं नमः
2. ॐ ऐं क्रूं नमः
3. ॐ ऐं श्रीं नमः
4. ॐ ऐं ह्लीं नमः
5. ॐ ऐं प्रें नमः
6. ॐ ऐं सौं नमः
7. ॐ ऐं स्हौं नमः
8. ॐ ऐं श्रूं नमः
9. ॐ ऐं क्लीं नमः
10. ॐ ऐं स्क्लीं नमः
11. ॐ ऐं प्रीं नमः
12. ॐ ऐं ग्लौं नमः
13. ॐ ऐं ह्स्ह्लीं नमः

14. ॐ ऐं स्तौं नमः

15. ॐ ऐं लीं नमः

16. ॐ ऐं ह्लीं नमः

17. ॐ ऐं स्तूं नमः

18. ॐ ऐं ज्स्हीं नमः

19. ॐ ऐं फ्रूं नमः

20. ॐ ऐं क्रूं नमः

21. ॐ ऐं ह्रीं नमः

22. ॐ ऐं ह्लूं नमः

23. ॐ ऐं क्ष्म्रीं नमः

24. ॐ ऐं श्रूं नमः

25. ॐ ऐं इं नमः

26. ॐ ऐं जुं नमः

27. ॐ ऐं त्रैं नमः

28. ॐ ऐं द्रूं नमः

29. ॐ ऐं ह्लौं नमः

30. ॐ ऐं क्लीं नमः

31. ॐ ऐं सूं नमः

32. ॐ ऐं हौं नमः

33. ॐ ऐं श्व्रं नमः

34. ॐ ऐं व्रूं नमः

35. ॐ ऐं फां नमः

36. ॐ ऐं ह्लीं नमः

37. ॐ ऐं लं नमः

38. ॐ ऐं ह्सौं नमः

39. ॐ ऐं सें नमः

40. ॐ ऐं ह्लीं नमः

41. ॐ ऐं ह्लौं नमः

42. ॐ ऐं विं नमः

43. ॐ ऐं प्लीं नमः

44. ॐ ऐं क्ष्म्क्लीं नमः

45. ॐ ऐं त्स्त्रां नमः

46. ॐ ऐं प्रं नमः

47. ॐ ऐं म्लीं नमः

48. ॐ ऐं स्त्रूं नमः

49. ॐ ऐं क्ष्मां नमः

50. ॐ ऐं स्तूं नमः

51. ॐ ऐं स्ह्रीं नमः

52. ॐ ऐं थ्प्रीं नमः

53. ॐ ऐं क्रौं नमः

54. ॐ ऐं श्रां नमः

55. ॐ ऐं म्लीं नमः

ॐ ऐं ह्रीं क्लीं श्रीं सौं नमः फट् स्वाहा

इत्येकादशोऽध्यायः

अथ द्वादशोऽध्यायः

1. ॐ ऐं ह्रीं नमः
2. ॐ ऐं ओं नमः
3. ॐ ऐं श्रीं नमः
4. ॐ ऐं ईं नमः
5. ॐ ऐं क्लीं नमः
6. ॐ ऐं क्रूं नमः
7. ॐ ऐं श्रूं नमः
8. ॐ ऐं प्रां नमः
9. ॐ ऐं क्रूं नमः
10. ॐ ऐं दिं नमः
11. ॐ ऐं फ्रें नमः
12. ॐ ऐं हं नमः
13. ॐ ऐं सः नमः

14. ॐ ऐं चें नमः

15. ॐ ऐं सूं नमः

16. ॐ ऐं प्रीं नमः

17. ॐ ऐं ब्लूं नमः

18. ॐ ऐं आं नमः

19. ॐ ऐं औं नमः

20. ॐ ऐं ह्रीं नमः

21. ॐ ऐं क्रीं नमः

22. ॐ ऐं द्रां नमः

23. ॐ ऐं श्रीं नमः

24. ॐ ऐं स्लीं नमः

25. ॐ ऐं क्लीं नमः

26. ॐ ऐं स्लूं नमः

27. ॐ ऐं ह्रीं नमः

28. ॐ ऐं ब्लीं नमः

29. ॐ ऐं त्रों नमः

30. ॐ ऐं ओं नमः

31. ॐ ऐं श्रौं नमः

32. ॐ ऐं ऐं नमः

33. ॐ ऐं प्रें नमः

34. ॐ ऐं द्रूं नमः

35. ॐ ऐं क्लूं नमः

36. ॐ ऐं औं नमः

37. ॐ ऐं सूं नमः

38. ॐ ऐं चें नमः

39. ॐ ऐं ह्रूं नमः

40. ॐ ऐं प्लीं नमः

41. ॐ ऐं क्षां नमः

ॐ यं यं यं रं रं रं ठं ठं ठं फट् स्वाहा

इति द्वादशोऽध्यायः

अथ त्रयोदशोऽध्यायः

1. ॐ ऐं श्रौं नमः
2. ॐ ऐं व्रीं नमः
3. ॐ ऐं ओं नमः
4. ॐ ऐं औं नमः
5. ॐ ऐं ह्लां नमः
6. ॐ ऐं श्रीं नमः
7. ॐ ऐं श्रां नमः
8. ॐ ऐं ओं नमः
9. ॐ ऐं प्लीं नमः
10. ॐ ऐं सौं नमः
11. ॐ ऐं ह्रीं नमः
12. ॐ ऐं क्रीं नमः
13. ॐ ऐं ह्लूं नमः

14. ॐ ऐं क्लीं नमः

15. ॐ ऐं ह्रीं नमः

16. ॐ ऐं प्लीं नमः

17. ॐ ऐं श्रीं नमः

18. ॐ ऐं ह्लीं नमः

19. ॐ ऐं श्रूं नमः

20. ॐ ऐं ह्रीं नमः

21. ॐ ऐं त्रूं नमः

22. ॐ ऐं ह्रीं नमः

23. ॐ ऐं ह्रां नमः

24. ॐ ऐं प्रीं नमः

25. ॐ ऐं ॐ नमः

26. ॐ ऐं सूं नमः

27. ॐ ऐं ह्रौं नमः

28. ॐ ऐं षौं नमः

29. ॐ ऐं आं ल्क्रीं नमः

30. ॐ ऐं ओं नमः

ऐं ह्रीं क्लीं चामुण्डायै विच्चे

इति त्रयोदशोऽध्यायः

इति तन्त्ररूपेणपरिणता

श्रीतन्त्रदुर्गासप्तशती समाप्त

तन्त्ररूपन्देवी सूक्तम्

1. ॐ ऐं ह्सौं नमः
2. ॐ ऐं ह्रीं नमः
3. ॐ ऐं श्रीं नमः
4. ॐ ऐं ह्रूं नमः
5. ॐ ऐं क्लीं नमः
6. ॐ ऐं रौं नमः
7. ॐ ऐं स्त्रीं नमः
8. ॐ ऐं म्लीं नमः
9. ॐ ऐं प्लूं नमः
10. ॐ ऐं स्हौं नमः
11. ॐ ऐं स्त्रीं नमः
12. ॐ ऐं ग्लूं नमः
13. ॐ ऐं व्रीं नमः

14. ॐ ऐं सौं नमः

15. ॐ ऐं लूं नमः

16. ॐ ऐं ल्लूं नमः

17. ॐ ऐं द्रां नमः

18. ॐ ऐं क्सां नमः

19. ॐ ऐं क्ष्म्रीं नमः

20. ॐ ऐं ग्लौं नमः

21. ॐ ऐं स्कं नमः

22. ॐ ऐं त्रूं नमः

23. ॐ ऐं स्क्लूं नमः

24. ॐ ऐं क्रौं नमः

25. ॐ ऐं श्रीं नमः

26. ॐ ऐं स्लूं नमः

27. ॐ ऐं क्लूं नमः

28. ॐ ऐं शां नमः

29. ॐ ऐं ल्हीं नमः

30. ॐ ऐं स्त्रूं नमः

31. ॐ ऐं ह्लीं नमः

32. ॐ ऐं ल्रीं नमः

33. ॐ ऐं सं नमः

34. ॐ ऐं ल्हूं नमः

35. ॐ ऐं ह्सूं नमः

36. ॐ ऐं श्रूं नमः

37. ॐ ऐं जूं नमः

38. ॐ ऐं ह्स्ल्रीं नमः

39. ॐ ऐं स्क्रीं नमः

40. ॐ ऐं क्लां नमः

41. ॐ ऐं श्रूं नम

42. ॐ ऐं हं नमः

43. ॐ ऐं ह्लीं नमः

44. ॐ ऐं क्स्त्रूं नमः

45. ॐ ऐं द्रौं नमः

46. ॐ ऐं क्लूं नमः

47. ॐ ऐं गां नमः

48. ॐ ऐं सं नमः

49. ॐ ऐं ल्स्त्रां नमः

50. ॐ ऐं फ्रीं नमः

51. ॐ ऐं स्लां नमः

52. ॐ ऐं ल्लूं नमः

53. ॐ ऐं फ्रें नमः

54. ॐ ऐं ओं नमः

55. ॐ ऐं स्म्लीं नमः

56. ॐ ऐं ह्लां नमः

57. ॐ ऐं ॐ नमः

58. ॐ ऐं ह्लूं नमः

59. ॐ ऐं हूं नमः

60. ॐ ऐं नं नमः

61. ॐ ऐं स्त्रां नमः

62. ॐ ऐं वं नमः

63. ॐ ऐं मं नमः

64. ॐ ऐं म्क्लीं नमः

65. ॐ ऐं शां नमः

66. ॐ ऐं लं नमः

67. ॐ ऐं भौं नमः

68. ॐ ऐं ल्लूं नमः

69. ॐ ऐं हौं नमः

70. ॐ ऐं ईं नमः

71. ॐ ऐं चें नमः

72. ॐ ऐं ल्क्रीं नमः

73. ॐ ऐं ह्लीं नमः

74. ॐ ऐं क्ष्म्ल्रीं नमः

75. ॐ ऐं पूं नमः

76. ॐ ऐं श्रौं नमः

77. ॐ ऐं ह्लौं नमः

78. ॐ ऐं भ्रूं नमः

79. ॐ ऐं क्स्त्रीं नमः

80. ॐ ऐं आं नमः

81. ॐ ऐं क्रूं नमः

82. ॐ ऐं त्रूं नमः

इति तन्त्ररूपन्देवीसूक्तम्

हरिविरञ्चिमहेश्वरपूजिताम्
भगवतीञ्जनदुर्गतिहारिणीम् ।
सकलतन्त्रमयीञ्जगदीश्वरीं
सुखमयीञ्जगताञ्जननीं भजे ॥ १ ॥

सर्वार्थसाधनकरीम्महतीमुदारां
स्वर्गापवर्गगतिदां करुणावताराम् ।
संसारतारणपरां हृतपापभारान्
दुर्गान्नमामि शिरसाऽहमनन्तसाराम् ॥ २ ॥

इति श्रीतन्त्रदुर्गासप्तशती
बीजनामावलि समाप्त

परमदेवी-सूक्तम्

ॐ अस्य श्रीपरमदेवतासूक्तमालामन्त्रस्य मार्कण्डेय सुमेधादि-ऋषयः। गायत्र्यादिनानाविधानि छन्दांसि। त्रिशक्तिरूपिणी चण्डिका देवता। ऐं बीजं सौः शक्तिः क्लीं कीलकं चतुर्विधपुरुषार्थसिध्यर्थे जपे विनियोगः ।

ॐ योगाढ्यामरकायनिर्गतमहत्तेजः समुत्पत्तिनी
भास्वत्पूर्णशशांकचारुवदना नीलोल्लसद्भ्रूलता ।
गौरोत्तुंगकुचद्वया तदुपरि स्फूर्जप्रभामण्डला
बन्धूकारुणकायकान्तिरवताच्छ्रीचण्डिका सर्वतः ॥

ॐ ऐं ह्रीं श्रीं ह्स्ख्फ्रें ह्सौं ह्सौः जय जय महालक्ष्मि जगदाधारवीजे सुरासुरत्रिभुवननिधाने दयाङ्कुरे सर्वतेजोरूपिणि महामहामहिमे महामहारूपिणि महामहामाये महामायास्वरूपिणि विरिञ्चसंस्तुते विधिवरदे चिदानन्दे (विद्यानन्दे) विष्णुदेहावृते

महामोहमोहिनि मधुकैटभजिघांसिनि

नित्यवरदानतत्परे महासुधाब्धिवासिनि

महामहत्तेजोधारिणि सर्वाधारे सर्वकारणकारणे

अचिन्त्यरूपे इन्द्रादिनिखिलनिर्जरसेविते

सामगानगायिनि पूर्णोदयकारिणि विजये जयन्ति

अपराजिते सर्वसुन्दरि रक्तांशुके सूर्यकोटिसंकाशे

चन्द्रकोटिसुशीतले अग्निकोटिदहनशीले यमकोटिक्रूरे

वायुकोटिवहनसुशीले ओंकारनादचिद्रूपे

निगमागममार्गदायिनि महिषासुरनिर्दलनि

धूम्रलोचनवधपरायणे चण्डमुण्डादिशिरश्छेदिनि

निखिलासुरबलखादिनि त्रिदशराज्यदायिनि

सर्वस्त्रीरत्नरूपिणि दिव्यदेहे निर्गुणे सदसद्रूपधारिणि

स्कन्दवरदे (सुरवरदे) भक्तत्राणतत्परे वरवरदे

सहस्रारे दशशताक्षरे अयुताक्षरे

सप्तकोटिचामुण्डारूपिणि नवकोटिकात्यायनिरूपिणि

अनेकशक्त्या लक्ष्यालक्ष्यस्वरूपे इन्द्राणि ब्रह्माणि
रुद्राणि कौमारि वैष्णावि वाराहि शिवदूति ईशानि
भीमे भ्रामरि नारसिंहि त्रयस्त्रिंशत्कोटिदैवते
अनन्तकोटिब्रह्माण्डनायिके
चतुरशीतिलक्षमुनिजनसंस्तुते सप्तकोटिमन्त्रस्वरूपे
महाकालरात्रिप्रकाशे कलाकाष्ठादिरूपिणि
चतुर्दशभुवनाविर्भवकारिणि गरुडगामिनि क्रौङ्कार
ह्रौङ्कार ह्रीङ्कार श्रीङ्कार क्षोङ्कार जूङ्कार सौङ्कार ऐङ्कार
क्लीङ्कार ह्लीङ्कार ह्लाङ्कार हौङ्कार नानाबीजमन्त्र
राजविराजित सकलसुन्दरीगणसेवित चरणारविन्दे
श्रीमहारात्रि त्रिपुरसुन्दरि कामेशदयिते
करुणारसकल्लोलिनि कल्पवृक्षाधःस्थिते
चिन्तामणिद्वीपादस्थित-मणिमन्दिरनिवासे चापिनि
खड्गिनि चक्रिणि गदिनि शङ्खिनि पद्मिनि
निखिलभैरवाराधिते समस्तयोगिनीचक्रपरिवृते कालि

कङ्कालि तारे तोतुले सुतारे ज्वालामुखि छिन्नमस्तके

भुवनेश्वरि त्रिपुरे त्रिलोकजननि

विष्णुवक्षःस्थलालङ्कारिणि अजिते अमिते अपराजिते

अनौपमचरिते गर्भवासादिदुःखापहारिणि

मुक्तिक्षेत्राधिष्ठायिनि शिवे शान्ति कुमारि देवि

देवीसूक्तसंस्तुते महाकालि महालक्ष्मि महासरस्वति

त्रयीविग्रहे प्रसीद प्रसीद सर्वमनोरथान् पूरय पूरय

सर्वारिष्टविघ्नांश्छेदय छेदय सर्वग्रहपीडाज्वरोग्रभयः

विध्वंसय विध्वंसय सद्यस्त्रिभुवनजीवजातं वशमानय

वशमानय मोक्षमार्गं दर्शय दर्शय ज्ञानमार्गं प्रकाशय

प्रकाशय अज्ञानतमो निरसय निरसय

धनधान्याभिवृद्धिं कुरु कुरु सर्वकल्याणानि कल्पय

कल्पय मां रक्ष रक्ष मम वज्रशरीरं साधय साधय

ऐं ह्रीं क्लीं चामुण्डायै विच्चे स्वाहा नमस्ते नमस्ते

नमस्ते स्वाहा ।

परं देव्या इदं सूक्तं यः पठेत्प्रयतो नरः ।
सर्वसिद्धिमवाप्नोति सर्वत्र विजयी भवेत् ॥ १ ॥

संग्रामेषु जपेच्छत्रून् मतङ्गानिव केसरी ।
वशयेन्निखिलान्लोकान् विशेषेण महीपतीन् ॥ २ ॥

त्रिकालं च पठेन्नित्यं देव्याः सूक्तमिदं परम् ।
तस्यविघ्नाः प्रलीयन्ते ग्रहपीडश्च दारुणाः ॥ ३ ॥

ज्वरादिरोगशमनं परकृत्यानिवारणम् ।
पराभिचारशमनं तीव्रदारिद्य नाशनम् ॥ ४ ॥

परकल्याणनिलयं देव्याः सन्तोषकारकम् ।
सहस्रावृत्तितो देवि मनोरथसिद्धिदम् ॥ ५ ॥

द्विसहस्रावृत्तिजपात्सर्वसंकष्टनाशनम् ।
त्रिसहस्रावृत्तितस्तु वशकृद्राजयोषिताम् ॥ ६ ॥

शतत्रयं पठेद्यस्तु वर्षत्रयमतन्द्रितः ।
स पश्येच्चण्डिकां साक्षाद् वरदानकृतोद्यमाम् ॥७॥

इदं रहस्यं परमं गोपनीयं प्रयत्नतः ।
न वाच्यं कस्यचिद्देवि निधानमिव सुन्दरि ॥८॥

॥ श्रीजगदम्बार्पणमस्तु ॥

॥ इति परमदेवी-सूक्तम् ॥

अपराजिता स्तोत्रम्

ॐ शुद्धस्फटिक-संकाशां चन्द्रकोटि सुशीतलाम् ।
अभय-वरदहस्तां शुक्लवस्त्रैरलंकृताम् ॥

नानाभरणसंयुक्तां चक्रवाकैश्च वेष्ठिताम् ।
एवं ध्यायेत् समासीनो य एतामपराजिताम् ॥

ॐ अस्य अपराजिता-मन्त्रस्य नारद वेदव्यास
ऋषिरनुष्टुप्छन्दः श्रीअपराजिता देवता लक्ष्मी बीजं
भुवनेश्वरी शक्तिर्मम सर्वाभीष्टसिद्ध्यर्थे जपे विनियोगः ।

मार्कण्डेय उवाच

श‍ृणुध्वं मुनयः सर्वे सर्वकामार्थसिद्धिदाम् ।
असिद्धसाधिनीं देवीं वैष्णवीमपराजिताम् ॥

ॐ नमो भगवते वासुदेवाय नमोऽस्त्वनन्ताय
सहस्रशीर्षाय क्षीरोदार्णवशायिने ।

शेषभोगपर्यंकाय गरुडवाहनाय अजाय अजिताय अमिताय अपराजिताय पीतवाससे वासुदेव शंकर्षण प्रद्युम्न अनिरुद्ध हयग्रीव महावराह नरसिंह वामन त्रिविक्रम राम राम श्रीराम मत्स्य कुर्म वरप्रद नमोऽस्तु ते स्वाहा ।

ॐ नमोऽस्तु ते सुर-दैत्य-दानव-नाग-गन्धर्व-यक्ष-राक्षस-भूत-प्रेत- पिशाच-कुष्माण्द-सिद्ध-योगिनी-डाकिनी-स्कन्द-पुरोगान् ग्रह नक्षत्रदोषान् दोषांश्चान्यान् हन हन दह दह पच पच मथ मथ विध्वंसय विध्वंसय विचूर्णय विचूर्णय विद्रावय विद्रावय शङ्खेन चक्रेण वज्रेण खड्गेन शूलेन गदया मूषलेन हलेन दामोदर भस्मीकुरु कुरु स्वाहा ।

ॐ सहस्त्रबाहो सहस्त्रप्रहरणायुध जय जय विजय विजय अजित अजित अमित अमित अपराजिता

अप्रतिहत सहस्त्रनेत्र ज्वल ज्वल प्रज्वल प्रज्वल विरूप विश्वरूप बहुरूप मधुसूदन महावराह अच्युत नृसिंह महापुरुष पुरुषोत्तम वैकुण्ठ नारायण पद्मनाभ गोविन्द अनिरुद्ध दामोदर हृषीकेश केशव वामन सर्वसुरोत्सादन सर्वभूतभयंकर सर्वशत्रुप्रमर्दन सर्वमन्त्र-प्रभञ्जन सर्वरोग-प्रणाशन सर्वनाग-प्रमर्दन सर्वदेव-महेश्वर सर्वबन्धविमोक्षण सर्वाहित-प्रमर्दन सर्वहिंस्त्रप्रदमन सर्वजरप्रणाशन सर्वग्रह-निवारण सर्वपापप्रमर्दन डाकिनीविध्वंसन सर्वदुःस्वप्ननाशन जनार्दन नमोऽस्तु ते स्वाहा ।

य ईमामपराजितां परमवैष्णवीं पठति विद्यां स्मरति सिद्धां महाविद्यां जपति पठति श्रृणोति स्मारयति धारयति कीर्त्तयति वाचयति वा गृहीत्वा हस्ते पथि गच्छति वा भक्त्या लिखित्वा गृहे स्थापयति वा तस्य नाग्नि-वायु-वज्रो-पलाऽशनिभयं न वर्षभयं न शत्रुभयं

न चोरभयं न सर्पभयं न स्वापदभयं न समुद्रभयं न राजभयं वा भवेत् ।

न तस्य रात्र्यन्धकार-स्त्री-राजकूल-विषोपविष गरलहन-वशीकरणविद्वेषणोच्चाटन-वध-बन्धनभयं वा भवेत् ।

ऐभिर्मन्त्रैरुदाहृतैः सिद्धैः संसिद्धपूजितैः ॥

तद्यथा ।

ॐ नमस्तेऽस्तु अभये अनघे अजिते अमिते अपरे अपराजिते पठति सिद्धे विद्ये स्मरति सिद्धे महाविद्ये ऐकानंशे उमे ध्रुवे अरुन्धति सावित्रि गायत्रि जातवेदसि मानस्तोके सरस्वति धमणि धामणि रमणि रामणि धरणि धारणि सौदामिनि अदिति दिति विनते गौरि गान्धारि शबरि किरातिनि मातंगि कृष्णे यषोदे सत्यवादिनि ब्रह्मवादिनि कालि कपालिनि

करालिनि करालनेत्रे भीमनादिनी विकरालनेत्रे
सद्योपचयकरि मातः सर्वयाचनवरदे शुभदे अर्थदे
साधिनि अपमृत्युं नाशय नाशय पापं हर हर जलगतं
स्थलगतं अन्तरीक्षगतं मां रक्ष रक्ष
सर्वभूतसर्वोपद्रवेभ्यः स्वाहा ।

यस्याः प्रणश्यते पुष्पं गर्भो वा पतते यदि ।
म्रियन्ते बालकाः यस्याः काकवन्ध्या च या भवेत् ॥

भूर्जपत्रे त्विमां विद्यां लिखित्वा धारयेत् सदा ।
ऐभिर्दोषैर्न लिप्येत शुभगा पुत्रिणी भवेत् ॥

भूर्जपत्रे कुंकुमेन लिखित्वा धारयेत्तु यः ।
रणे राजकूले द्यूते संग्रामे रिपुसंकुले ॥

अग्निचौरभये घोरे नित्यं तस्य जयो भवेत् ।
शस्त्रञ्च वारयत्येषा समये काण्डधारिणी ॥

गुल्म-शूलाक्षिरोगाणां क्षिप्रं नाशयते व्यथाम् ।
शिरोरोगज्वराणाञ्च नाशिनीं सर्वदेहिनाम् ॥

तद्यथा ।

ऐकाहिक-द्व्याहिक-त्र्याहिक-चातुर्थिक-मासिक-
द्वैमासिक-त्रैमासिक-चातुर्मासिक-षाणमासिक-
मौहूर्त्तिक-वातिक-पैत्तिक-श्लैष्मिक-सान्निपातिक-ज्वर
सततज्वर-सन्तत-ज्वर विषमज्वर-
ग्रहनक्षत्रदोषांश्चान्यान् हर हर कालि शर शर गौरि
धम धम विद्ये आले माले ताले बन्धे पच पच विद्ये
मथ मथ विद्ये नाशय नाशय पापं हर हर दुःस्वप्नं
विध्वंसय विध्वंसय विघ्नविनाशिनि रजनि सन्ध्ये
दुन्दुभिनादे मानस्तोके मानसवेगे शङ्खिणि चक्रिणि
वज्रिणि गदिनि शूलिनि अपमृत्यु-विनाशिनि विश्वेश्वरि
द्रविढि द्राविढि केशवदयिते पशुपतिसहिते दुःखदुरन्ते
दुन्दुभिनादिनि भीममर्दिनि दमनि दामिनि शबरि

किराति मातंगि माहेश्वरि इन्द्राणि ब्रह्माणि वाराहि
माहेन्द्रि कौमारि चण्डि चामुण्डे नमोऽस्तु ते ।

ॐ ह्राँ ह्रीँ ह्रूँ ह्रैँ ह्रौँ ह्रः तुरु तुरु स्वाहा ।
ये मां द्विषन्ति प्रत्यक्षं परोक्षं वा तान् सर्वान् हन हन
दह दह पच पच मर्दय मर्दय तापय तापय शोषय
शोषय उत्सादय उत्सादय ब्रह्माणि वैष्णवि माहेश्वरि
वाराहि कौमारि वैनायकि ऐन्द्रि आग्नेयि चण्डि
चामुण्डे वारुणि वायवि सर्वकामफलप्रदे रक्ष रक्ष
प्रचण्डविद्ये इन्द्रोपेन्द्र-भगिनि जये विजये शान्ति
पुष्टि-तुष्टि-कीर्त्तिविवर्द्धिनि कामांकुशे कामदुघे
सर्वकामवरप्रदे सर्वभूतेषु मां प्रियं कुरु कुरु स्वाहा ।

ॐ ह्रीँ ह्रीँ ह्रूँ ह्रः ।

ॐ आकर्षिणि आवेशिनि ज्वालामालिनि रमणि
रामणि धमनि धामनि तपनि तापनि मादनोन्मादिनि

संशोषिणि महाकालि नीलपताके महारात्रि महागौरि
महामाये महाश्रये महाचान्द्रि महाशौरि महामयुरि
आदित्यरश्मि जाह्नवि यमघण्टे ।

ॐ आं किलिकिलि चिन्तामणि सुरभि-सुरोत्पन्ने
सर्वकामदुघे यथाभिलाषितं कार्यं तन्मे सिध्यतु
स्वाहा ।

ॐ आदिते स्वाहा ॐ अपराजिते स्वाहा
ॐ भूः स्वाहा ॐ भुवः स्वाहा ॐ स्वः स्वाहा
ॐ भूर्भुवः स्वः स्वाहा ।

षत एवागतं पापं तत्रैव प्रतिगच्छतु स्वाहा ।
ॐ बले बले महाबले असिद्धसाधिनि स्वाहा ॥

॥ ॐ इति विष्णुधर्मोत्तरे तृतीयकाण्डे त्रैलोक्य-
विजया-नामापराजिता-स्तोत्रं समाप्तम् ॐ ॥

श्रीकुञ्जिकास्तोत्रम्

श्री गणेशाय नमः

ॐ अस्य श्रीकुञ्जिकास्तोत्रमन्त्रस्य सदाशिव ऋषिः अनुष्टुप् छन्दः श्रीत्रिगुणात्मिका देवता ॐ ऐं बीजं ॐ ह्रीं शक्तिः ॐ क्लीं कीलकं मम सर्वाभीष्टसिद्ध्यर्थे जपे विनियोगः ।

शिव उवाच

श्रृणु देव प्रवक्ष्यामि कुञ्जिकास्तोत्रमुत्तमम् ।
येन मन्त्रप्रभावेण चण्डीजापः शुभो भवेत् ॥ १ ॥

न कवचं नार्गलास्तोत्रं कीलकं न रहस्यकम् ।
न सूक्तं नापि वा ध्यानं न न्यासो न वार्चनम् ॥ २ ॥

कुञ्जिकापाठमात्रेण दुर्गापाठफलं लभेत् ।
अतिगुह्यतरं देवि देवानामपि दुर्लभम् ॥ ३ ॥

गोपनीयं प्रयत्नेन स्वयोनिरिव पार्वति ।
मारणं मोहनं वश्यं स्तम्भनोच्चाटनादिकम् ॥४॥

पाठमात्रेण संसिध्येत् कुञ्जिकास्तोत्रमुत्तमम् ।
ॐ श्रूं श्रूं श्रूं शं फट् ऐं ह्रीं क्लीं ज्वल उज्ज्वल प्रज्वल
ह्रीं ह्रीं क्लीं स्त्रवय स्त्रावय शापं नाशय नाशय श्रीं श्रीं
श्रीं जूं सः स्त्रावय आदय स्वाहा ॥५॥

ॐ श्लीं हूं क्लीं ग्लां जूं सः ज्वल उज्ज्वल मन्त्रं प्रज्वल
हं सं लं क्षं फट् स्वाहा ।
नमस्ते रुद्ररूपायै नमस्ते मधुमर्दिनि ॥६॥

नमस्ते कैटभनाशिन्यै नमस्ते महिषार्दिनि ।
नमस्ते शुम्भहन्त्र्यै च निशुम्भासुरसूदिनि ॥७॥

नमस्ते जाग्रते देवि जपे सिद्धिं कुरूष्व मे ।
ऐङ्कारी सृष्टिरूपिण्यै ह्रीङ्कारी प्रतिपालिका ॥८॥

क्लीं काली कालरूपिण्यै बीजरूपे नमोऽस्तु ते ।
चामुण्डा चण्डरूपा च यैङ्कारी वरदायिनी ॥९॥

विच्चे त्वभयदा नित्यं नमस्ते मन्त्ररूपिणि ।
धां धीं धूं धूर्जटेः पत्नी वां वीं वागीश्वरी तथा ॥१०॥

क्रां क्रीं क्रूं कुञ्जिका देवि श्रां श्रीं श्रूं मे शुभं कुरु ।
हूं हूं हूङ्काररूपिण्यै ज्रां ज्रीं ज्रूं भालनादिनी ॥११॥

भ्रां भ्रीं भ्रूं भैरवी भद्रे भवान्यै ते नमो नमः ।
ॐ अं कं चं टं तं पं सां विदुरां विदुरां विमर्दय विमर्दय
ह्रीं क्षां क्षीं स्त्रीं जीवय जीवय त्रोटय त्रोटय जम्भय
जम्भय दीपय दीपय मोचय मोचय हूं फट् ज्रां वौषट्
ऐं ह्रीं क्लीं रञ्जय रञ्जय सञ्जय सञ्जय गुञ्जय गुञ्जय
बन्धय बन्धय भ्रां भ्रीं भ्रूं भैरवी भद्रे सङ्कुच सङ्कुच
त्रोटय त्रोटय म्लीं स्वाहा ॥१२॥

पां पीं पूं पार्वती पूर्णा खां खीं खूं खेचरी तथा ।
म्लां म्लीं म्लूं मूलवस्तीर्णा कुञ्जिकास्तोत्रहेतवे ॥१३॥

अभक्ताय न दातव्यं गोपितं रक्ष पार्वति ।
विहीना कुञ्जिकादेव्या यस्तु सप्तशतीं पठेत् ॥१४॥

न तस्य जायते सिद्धिर्ह्यरण्ये रुदितं यथा ॥१५॥

॥ इति श्रीडामरतन्त्रे ईश्वरपार्वतीसंवादे
कुञ्जिकास्तोत्रं सम्पूर्णम् ॥

देविपुष्पाञ्जलीस्तोत्रम्

अयि गिरिनन्दिनि नन्दितमेदिनि विश्वविनोदिनि नन्दिनुते
गिरिवरविन्ध्यशिरोऽधिनिवासिनि विष्णुविलासिनि जिष्णुनुते ।
भगवति हे शितिकण्ठकुटुम्बिनि भूरिकुटुम्बिनि भूतिकृते
जय जय हे महिषासुरमर्दिनि रम्यकपर्दिनि शैलसुते
॥ १ ॥

सुरवरवर्षिणि दुर्धरधर्षिणि दुर्मुखमर्षिणि हर्षरते
त्रिभुवनपोषिणि शङ्करतोषिणि कल्मषमोषिणि घोषरते ।
दनुजनिरोषिणि दुर्मदशोषिणि दुर्मुनिरोषिनि सिन्धुसुते
जय जय हे महिषासुरमर्दिनि रम्यकपर्दिनि शैलसुते
॥ २ ॥

अयि जगदम्ब कदम्बवन प्रियवासिनि तोषिणि हासरते
शिखरिशिरोमणितुङ्ग हिमालयश्रृङ्गनिजालयमध्यगते ।
मधुमधुरे मधुकैटभगञ्जिनि महिषविदारिणि रासरते
जय जय हे महिषासुरमर्दिनि रम्यकपर्दिनि शैलसुते ॥ ३ ॥

अयि निजहुँकृतिमात्रनिराकृतधूम्रविलोचनधूम्रशते
समरविशोषितरोषितशोणितबीजसमुद्भवबीजलते ।
शिवशिवशुम्भनिशुम्भमहाहवतर्पितभूतपिशाचरते
जय जय हे महिषासुरमर्दिनि रम्यकपर्दिनि शैलसुते
॥४॥

अयि शतखण्डविखण्डितरुण्डवितुण्डितशुण्डगजाधिपते
निजभुजदण्डनिपातितचण्डविपाटितमुण्डभटाधिपते ।
रिपुगजगण्डविदारणचण्डपराक्रमशौण्डमृगाधिपते
जय जय हे महिषासुरमर्दिनि रम्यकपर्दिनि शैलसुते
॥५॥

धनुरनुषङ्ग रनक्षणसङ्ग परिस्फुरदङ्गनटत्कटके
कनकपिशङ्गपुष्पत्कनिषङ्गरसद्भटशृङ्गहताबटुके ।
हतचतुरङ्गबलक्षितिरङ्गघटद्बहुरङ्गरटद्बटुके
जय जय हे महिषासुरमर्दिनि रम्यकपर्दिनि शैलसुते
॥६॥

अयि रणदुर्मदशत्रुवधाद्धुरदुर्धरनिर्भरशक्तिभृते
चतुरविचारधुरीणमहाशयदूतकृतप्रमथाधिपते ।
दुरितदुरीहदुराशयदुर्मतिदानवदूतदुरन्तगते
जय जय हे महिषासुरमर्दिनि रम्यकपर्दिनि शैलसुते
॥७॥

अयि शरणागतवैरिवधूजनवीरवराभयदायिकरे
त्रिभुवनमस्तकशूलविरोधिशिरोधिकृतामलशूलकरे ।
दुमिदुमितामरदुन्दुभिनादमुहुर्मुखरीकृतदिङ्गिकरे
जय जय हे महिषासुरमर्दिनि रम्यकपर्दिनि शैलसुते
॥८॥

सुरललनाततथेयितथेयितथाभिनयोत्तरनृत्यरते
कृतकुकुथाकुकुथोदिडदाडिकतालकुतूहलगानरते ।
धुधुकुटधूधुटधिन्धिमितध्वनिधिरमृदङ्गनिनादरते
जय जय हे महिषासुरमर्दिनि रम्यकपर्दिनि शैलसुते
॥९॥

जय जय जाप्यजये जयशब्दपरस्तुतितत्परविश्वनुते
झणझणझिंझिमझिंकृतनूपुरशिञ्जितमोहितभूतपते ।
नटितनटार्धनटीनटनायकनाटननाटितनट्यरते
जय जय हे महिषासुरमर्दिनि रम्यकपर्दिनि शैलसुते
॥१०॥

अयि सुमनःसुमनःसुमनःसुमनःसुमनोरमकान्तियुते
श्रितरजनीरजनीरजनीरजनीरजनीकरवक्त्रभृते ।
सुनयनविभ्रमरभ्रमरभ्रमरभ्रमरभ्रमराभिद्दते
जय जय हे महिषासुरमर्दिनि रम्यकपर्दिनि शैलसुते
॥११॥

महितमहाहवमल्लमतल्लिकवल्लितरल्लितभल्लिरते
विरचितबल्लिकपालिकपल्लिकझिल्लिकभिल्लिकवर्गवृते ।
श्रुतकृतपुल्लसमुल्लसितारुणतल्लजपल्लवसल्ललिते
जय जय हे महिषासुरमर्दिनि रम्यकपर्दिनि शैलसुते
॥१२॥

अयि सुदतीजनलालसमानसमोहनमन्मथराजसुते
अविरलगण्डगलन्मदमेदुरमत्तमतङ्गजराजगते ।
त्रिभुवनभूषणभूतकलानिधिरूपपयोनिधिराजसुते
जय जय हे महिषासुरमर्दिनि रम्यकपर्दिनि शैलसुते
॥ १३ ॥

कमलदलामलकोमलकान्तिकलाकलितामलभालतले
सकलविलासकलानिलयक्रमकेलिचलत्कलहंसकुले ।
अलिकुलसङ्कुलकुन्तलमण्डलमौलिमिलद्बकुलालिकुले
जय जय हे महिषासुरमर्दिनि रम्यकपर्दिनि शैलसुते
॥ १४ ॥

करमुरलीरववीर्जितकूजितलज्जितकोकिलमञ्जुमते
मिलितमिलिन्दमनोहरगुञ्जितरञ्जितशैलनिकुञ्जगते ।
निजगणभूतमहाशबरीगणरङ्गणसम्भृतकेलिरते
जय जय हे महिषासुरमर्दिनि रम्यकपर्दिनि शैलसुते
॥ १५ ॥

कटितटपीतदुकूलविचित्रमयूखतिरस्कृतचण्डरुचे
जितकनकाचलमौलिमदोर्जित गर्जितकुञ्जरकुम्भकुचे ।
प्रणतसुराऽसुरमौलिमणिस्फुरदंशुलसन्नखचन्द्ररुचे
जय जय हे महिषासुरमर्दिनि रम्यकपर्दिनि शैलसुते
॥ १६ ॥

विजितसहस्रकरैकसहस्रकरैकसहस्रकरैकनुते
कृतसुरतारकसङ्गरतारकसङ्गरतारकसूनुनुते ।
सुरथसमाधिसमानसमाधिसमान समाधिसुजाप्यरते
जय जय हे महिषासुरमर्दिनि रम्यकपर्दिनि शैलसुते
॥ १७ ॥

पदकमलं करुणानिलये वरिवस्यति योऽनुदिनं सुशिवे
अयि कमले कमलानिलये कमलानिलयः स कथं न भवेत् ।
तव पदमेव परं पदमस्त्विति शीलयतो मम किं न शिवे
जय जय हे महिषासुरमर्दिनि रम्यकपर्दिनि शैलसुते
॥ १८ ॥

कनकलसत्कलशीकजलैरनुषिञ्चति तेऽङ्गणरंगभुवम्
भजति स किं न शचीकुचकुम्भनटीपरिरम्भसुखानुभवम् ।
तव चरणं शरणं करवाणि सुवाणि पथं मम देहि शिवम्
जय जय हे महिषासुरमर्दिनि रम्यकपर्दिनि शैलसुते
॥१९॥

तव विमलेन्दुकुलं वदनेन्दुमलं कलयन्ननुकूलयते
किमु पुरुहूतपुरीन्दुमुखीसुमुखीभिरसौ विमुखीक्रियते ।
मम तु मतं शिवमानधने भवती कृपया किमु न क्रियते
जय जय हे महिषासुरमर्दिनि रम्यकपर्दिनि शैलसुते
॥२०॥

अयि मयि दीनदयालुतया कृपयैव त्वया भवितव्यमुमे
अयि जगतो जननीति यथाऽसि मयाऽसि तथाऽनुमतासि रमे
यदुचितमत्र भवत्पुरगं कुरु शाम्भवि देवि दयां कुरु मे
जय जय हे महिषासुरमर्दिनि रम्यकपर्दिनि शैलसुते
॥२१॥

स्तुतिमिमां स्तिमितः सुससमाधिना
नियमतो यमतोऽनुदिनं पठेत् ।
परमया रमया स निषेव्यते
परिजनोऽरिजनोऽपि च तं भजेत् ॥ २२॥

॥ इति देविपुष्पाञ्जलिस्तोत्रं समाप्तम् ॥

चण्डी माँ की आरती

जय चण्डी जय जय (माँ) जय चण्डी जय जय
भयहारिणि भवतारिणि भवभामिनि जय जय
ॐ जय चण्डी जय जय

तू ही सत-चित-सुखमय शुद्ध ब्रह्मरूपा (माँ)
सत्य सनातन सुन्दर पर-शिव सूर-भूपा
ॐ जय चण्डी जय जय ॥ १ ॥

आदि अनादि अनामय अविचल अविनाशी (माँ)
अमल अनन्त अगोचर अज आनन्दराशी
ॐ जय चण्डी जय जय ॥ २ ॥

अविकारी अघहारी अकल कलाधारी (माँ)
कर्त्ता विधि भर्त्ता हरि हर संहरकारी
ॐ जय चण्डी जय जय ॥ ३ ॥

तू विधि वधू रमा तू उमा महामाया (माँ)
मूलप्रकृति विद्या तू तू जननी जाया
ॐ जय चण्डी जय जय ॥४॥

राम कृष्ण तू सीता ब्रजरानी राधा (माँ)
तू वाञ्छाकल्पद्रुम हारिणि सब बाधा
ॐ जय चण्डी जय जय ॥५॥

दश विद्या नव दुर्गा नानाशस्त्रकरा (माँ)
अष्टमातृका योगिनि नव नव रूप धरा
ॐ जय चण्डी जय जय ॥६॥

तू परधामनिवासिनि महाविलासिनि तू (माँ)
तु ही श्मशानविहारिणि ताण्डवलासिनि तू
ॐ जय चण्डी जय जय ॥७॥

सुर मुनि मोहिनि सौम्या तू शोभाऽऽधारा (माँ)
विवसनविकट-सरूपा प्रलयमयी धारा
ॐ जय चण्डी जय जय ॥८॥

तू ही स्नेह-सुधामयि तू अति गरलमना (माँ)
रत्नविभूषित तू ही तू ही अस्थि तना
ॐ जय चण्डी जय जय ॥९॥

मूलाधारनिवासिनि इह पर सिद्धि प्रदे (माँ)
कालातीता काली कमल तू वरदे
ॐ जय चण्डी जय जय ॥१०॥

शक्ति शक्ति धर तू ही नित्य अभेदमयी (माँ)
भेदप्रदर्शिनि वाणी विमले वेदत्रयी
ॐ जय चण्डी जय जय ॥११॥

हम् अति दीन दुखी (माँ) विपत्-जाल घेरे (माँ)
हैं कपूत् अति कपटी पर बालक तेरे
ॐ जय चण्डी जय जय ॥१२॥

निज स्वभाववश जननी दया दृष्टि कीजै (माँ)
करुणा कर करुणामयि चरण-शरण दीजै
ॐ जय चण्डी जय जय ॥१३॥

जय चण्डी जय जय (माँ) जय चण्डी जय जय
भयहारिणि भवतारिणि भवभामिनि जय जय
ॐ जय चण्डी जय जय

देवीमयी

तव च का किल न स्तुतिरम्बिके
सकलशब्दमयीकिल ते तनुः ।
निखिलमूर्तिषु मे भवदन्वयो
मनसिजासु बहिःप्रसरासु च ॥

इति विचिन्त्य शिवे शमिताशिवे
जगति जातमयत्नवशादिदम् ।
स्तुतिजपार्चनचिन्तनवर्जिता
न खलु काचन कालकलास्ति मे ॥

भगवतीस्तुतिः

प्रातः स्मरामि शरदिन्दुकरोज्ज्वलाभां
सद्रत्नवन्मकरकुण्डलहारभूषाम् ।
दिव्यायुधोजितसुनीलसहस्रहस्तां
रक्तोत्पलाभचरणां भवतीं परेशाम् ॥

प्रातर्नमामि महिषासुरचण्डमुण्ड-
शुम्भासुरप्रमुखदैत्यविनाशदक्षाम् ।
ब्रह्मेन्द्ररुद्रमुनिमोहनशीललीलां
चण्डीं समस्तसुरमूर्तिमनेकरूपाम् ॥

प्रातर्भजामि भजतामभिलाषदात्रीं
धात्रीं समस्तजगतां दुरितापहन्त्रीम् ।
संसारबन्धनवमोचनहेतुभूतां
मायां परां समधिगम्य परस्य विष्णोः ॥

प्रणामः

ॐ दुर्गां शिवां शान्तिकरीं ब्रह्माणीं ब्रह्मणः प्रियां ।
सर्वलोक प्रणेत्रीञ्च प्रणमामि सदा शिवाम् ॥

मङ्गलां शोभनां शुद्धां निष्कलां परमां कलाम् ।
विश्वेश्वरीं विश्वमातां चण्डिकां प्रणमाम्यहम् ॥

सर्वदेवमयीं देवीं सर्वरोगभयापहाम् ।
ब्रह्मेशविष्णुनमितां प्रणमामि सदाशिवां ॥

विन्ध्यस्थां विन्ध्यनिलयां दिव्यस्थाननिवासिनीम् ।
योगिनीं योगजननीं चण्डिकां प्रणमाम्यहम् ॥

ईशानमातरं देवीमीश्वरीमीश्वरप्रियाम् ।
प्रणतोऽस्मि सदादुर्गां संसारार्णवतारिणीम् ॥

ॐ महादेव महात्राण महायोगि महेश्वर ।
सर्वपापहरां देव मकाराय नमो नमः ॥

ॐ नमः शिवाय शान्ताय कारणत्रय हेतवे ।
निवेदयामि चात्मानं त्वं गतिः परमेश्वर ॥

॥ इति संस्कृतम् बीजमन्त्रात्मक
तन्त्रदुर्गासप्तशती सम्पूर्णम् ॥

आदिशक्तये नमः

ādiśaktaye namaḥ

We bow to the Foremost Energy

श्रीतन्त्रदुर्गासप्तशती

śrītantradurgāsaptaśatī

The Respected Integration of the Seven Hundred
Verses of She Who Removes All Difficulties

विश्वेश्वरीं विश्वमयीं

विरूपामज्ञानहन्त्रीं विमलस्वरूपाम् ।

शश्वत्प्रसन्नाङ्करुणावतारान्

तन्त्रस्वरूपाञ्चनमामिदुर्गाम् ॥ १ ॥

viśveśvarīṃ viśvamayīṃ

virūpāmajñānahantrīṃ vimalasvarūpām ।

śaśvatprasannāṅkaruṇāvatārān

tantrasvarūpāñcanamāmidurgām ॥ 1 ॥

I bow to the Reliever of Difficulties, to the Ruler of the Universe, to She who embodies the Universe, to She who destroys corruption and ignorance, Whose intrinsic nature is pure or without blemish; To the eternally pleasing incarnations of compassion, and to She whose intrinsic nature is to weave together.

चिदानन्दरूपे हरीशादिवन्द्ये

सदामन्दहासे जगद्भीतिनाशे ।

चिदानन्ददेत्वञ्च तन्त्रस्वरूपेजनं

पाहिदीनन्तवार्चाविहीनम् ॥ २ ॥

cidānandarūpe harīśādivandye

sadāmandahāse jagadbhītināśe I

cidānandadetvañca tantrasvarūpejanaṃ

pāhidīnantavārcāvihīnam II2II

The form of infinite consciousness and bliss, who is praised by Viṣṇu and others, who always smiles gently in delight, who destroys the fears of the world, and whose intrinsic nature moves people towards weaving together consciousness and bliss; Protect your children who are in despair, who always offer your praise.

नजानातिविष्णुःशिवोनैववेत्तिस्वयम्भूः

स्वयन्नैवजानातिमातः ।

चरित्रन्दयाधारिके ते विचित्रङ्कथन्मन्द

बुद्धिर्जनःस्यात्समर्थ॥ ३ ॥

najānātiviṣṇuḥśivonaivavettisvayambhūḥ

svayannaivajānātimātaḥ I

caritrandayādhārike te vicitraṅkathanmanda

buddhirjanaḥsyātsamartha II3II

Who is unknown to Viṣhṇu, Śiva, Svayambhū, even unknown to Herself, the Unknowable Mother whose activities demonstrate compassion. The intelligent people who recite those stories delight in the increase of their capacity.

तथाप्यम्बलोलोपकारायलोकेचरित्रं

वदाम्यत्रकिञ्चित्प्रसिद्धम् ।

तवप्रेरणैवाभवद्धेतुभूतामदीयेहृदब्जे

महादेविदुर्गे॥ ४ ॥

tathāpyambalolopakārāyalokecaritraṃ vadāmyatrakiñcitprasiddham I tavapreraṇaivābhavadhetubhūtāmadīyehṛdabje mahādevidurge II4II

In this way the Mother gives benefit to whomever recites Her stories and makes even some of Her glorious activities known. Oh Great Goddess who Removes all Difficulties, You are the cause of all being and the motivation for all action; I offer my heart to you in praise!

तन्त्ररूपं रात्रिसूक्तम् tantrarūpaṃ rātrisūktam

1	ॐ ऐं ब्लूं नमः	oṃ aiṃ blūṃ namaḥ
2	ॐ ऐं ठां नमः	oṃ aiṃ ṭhāṃ namaḥ
3	ॐ ऐं ह्रीं नमः	oṃ aiṃ hrīṃ namaḥ
4	ॐ ऐं स्रां नमः	oṃ aiṃ srāṃ namaḥ
5	ॐ ऐं स्लूं नमः	oṃ aiṃ slūṃ namaḥ
6	ॐ ऐं क्रैं नमः	oṃ aiṃ kraiṃ namaḥ
7	ॐ ऐं त्रां नमः	oṃ aiṃ trāṃ namaḥ
8	ॐ ऐं फ्रां नमः	oṃ aiṃ phrāṃ namaḥ
9	ॐ ऐं जीं नमः	oṃ aiṃ jīṃ namaḥ
10	ॐ ऐं लूं नमः	oṃ aiṃ lūṃ namaḥ
11	ॐ ऐं स्लूं नमः	oṃ aiṃ slūṃ namaḥ
12	ॐ ऐं नों नमः	oṃ aiṃ noṃ namaḥ
13	ॐ ऐं स्त्रीं नमः	oṃ aiṃ strīṃ namaḥ
14	ॐ ऐं प्रूं नमः	oṃ aiṃ prūṃ namaḥ
15	ॐ ऐं स्रूं नमः	oṃ aiṃ srūṃ namaḥ
16	ॐ ऐं जां नमः	oṃ aiṃ jāṃ namaḥ

17	ॐ ऐं वौं नमः	oṃ aiṃ vauṃ namaḥ
18	ॐ ऐं ओं नमः	oṃ aiṃ oṃ namaḥ

इति तन्त्ररूपं रात्रिसूक्तम्

iti tantrarūpaṃ rātrisūktam

Here ends the Tantrik Form of the Praise to the Night of Duality

ॐ ऐं ह्रीं क्लीं चामुण्डायै विच्चे

aiṃ hrīṃ klīṃ cāmuṇḍāyai vicce

ॐ बीजत्रयायैविद्महे तत्प्रधानायैधीमहि

तन्नः शक्तिः प्राचोदयात्

oṃ bījatrayāyai vidmahe
tatpradhānāyai dhīmahi
tantraḥ śaktiḥ prācodayāt

Oṃ the infinite beyond conception,
we contemplate She who embodies the Three Bijas,
meditate upon That which is Highest and Foremost,
may that Energy grant us increase.

अथ प्रथमोऽध्यायः atha prathamo-dhyāyaḥ

1	ॐ ऐं श्रीं नमः	oṃ aiṃ śrīṃ namaḥ
2	ॐ ऐं ह्रीं नमः	oṃ aiṃ hrīṃ namaḥ
3	ॐ ऐं क्लीं नमः	oṃ aiṃ klīṃ namaḥ
4	ॐ ऐं श्रीं नमः	oṃ aiṃ śrīṃ namaḥ
5	ॐ ऐं प्रीं नमः	oṃ aiṃ prīṃ namaḥ
6	ॐ ऐं ह्रां नमः	oṃ aiṃ hrāṃ namaḥ
7	ॐ ऐं ह्रीं नमः	oṃ aiṃ hrīṃ namaḥ
8	ॐ ऐं सौं नमः	oṃ aiṃ sauṃ namaḥ
9	ॐ ऐं प्रें नमः	oṃ aiṃ preṃ namaḥ
10	ॐ ऐं म्रीं नमः	oṃ aiṃ mrīṃ namaḥ
11	ॐ ऐं ह्लीं नमः	oṃ aiṃ hlīṃ namaḥ
12	ॐ ऐं म्लीं नमः	oṃ aiṃ mlīṃ namaḥ
13	ॐ ऐं स्त्रीं नमः	oṃ aiṃ strīṃ namaḥ
14	ॐ ऐं क्रां नमः	oṃ aiṃ krāṃ namaḥ
15	ॐ ऐं ह्स्लीं नमः	oṃ aiṃ hslīṃ namaḥ
16	ॐ ऐं क्रीं नमः	oṃ aiṃ krīṃ namaḥ
17	ॐ ऐं चां नमः	oṃ aiṃ cāṃ namaḥ
18	ॐ ऐं में नमः	oṃ aiṃ meṃ namaḥ
19	ॐ ऐं क्रीं नमः	oṃ aiṃ krīṃ namaḥ
20	ॐ ऐं वैं नमः	oṃ aiṃ vaiṃ namaḥ

21	ॐ ऐं ह्रौं नमः	oṃ aiṃ hrauṃ namaḥ
22	ॐ ऐं युं नमः	oṃ aiṃ yuṃ namaḥ
23	ॐ ऐं जुं नमः	oṃ aiṃ juṃ namaḥ
24	ॐ ऐं हं नमः	oṃ aiṃ haṃ namaḥ
25	ॐ ऐं शं नमः	oṃ aiṃ śaṃ namaḥ
26	ॐ ऐं रौं नमः	oṃ aiṃ rauṃ namaḥ
27	ॐ ऐं यं नमः	oṃ aiṃ yaṃ namaḥ
28	ॐ ऐं विं नमः	oṃ aiṃ viṃ namaḥ
29	ॐ ऐं वैं नमः	oṃ aiṃ vaiṃ namaḥ
30	ॐ ऐं चें नमः	oṃ aiṃ ceṃ namaḥ
31	ॐ ऐं ह्रीं नमः	oṃ aiṃ hrīṃ namaḥ
32	ॐ ऐं क्रं नमः	oṃ aiṃ kraṃ namaḥ
33	ॐ ऐं सं नमः	oṃ aiṃ saṃ namaḥ
34	ॐ ऐं कं नमः	oṃ aiṃ kaṃ namaḥ
35	ॐ ऐं श्रीं नमः	oṃ aiṃ śrīṃ namaḥ
36	ॐ ऐं त्रौं नमः	oṃ aiṃ trauṃ namaḥ
37	ॐ ऐं स्त्रां नमः	oṃ aiṃ strāṃ namaḥ
38	ॐ ऐं ज्यैं नमः	oṃ aiṃ jyaiṃ namaḥ
39	ॐ ऐं रौं नमः	oṃ aiṃ rauṃ namaḥ
40	ॐ ऐं द्रां नमः	oṃ aiṃ drāṃ namaḥ
41	ॐ ऐं द्रों नमः	oṃ aiṃ droṃ namaḥ

42	ॐ ऐं ह्रां नमः	oṃ aiṃ hrāṃ namaḥ
43	ॐ ऐं द्रूं नमः	oṃ aiṃ drūṃ namaḥ
44	ॐ ऐं शां नमः	oṃ aiṃ śāṃ namaḥ
45	ॐ ऐं मीं नमः	oṃ aiṃ mīṃ namaḥ
46	ॐ ऐं श्रौं नमः	oṃ aiṃ śrauṃ namaḥ
47	ॐ ऐं जुं नमः	oṃ aiṃ juṃ namaḥ
48	ॐ ऐं ह्लूं नमः	oṃ aiṃ hlrūṃ namaḥ
49	ॐ ऐं श्रूं नमः	oṃ aiṃ śrūṃ namaḥ
50	ॐ ऐं प्रीं नमः	oṃ aiṃ prīṃ namaḥ
51	ॐ ऐं रं नमः	oṃ aiṃ raṃ namaḥ
52	ॐ ऐं वं नमः	oṃ aiṃ vaṃ namaḥ
53	ॐ ऐं ब्रीं नमः	oṃ aiṃ brīṃ namaḥ
54	ॐ ऐं ब्लं नमः	oṃ aiṃ blaṃ namaḥ
55	ॐ ऐं स्त्रौं नमः	oṃ aiṃ strauṃ namaḥ
56	ॐ ऐं ल्वां नमः	oṃ aiṃ lvāṃ namaḥ
57	ॐ ऐं लूं नमः	oṃ aiṃ lūṃ namaḥ
58	ॐ ऐं सां नमः	oṃ aiṃ sāṃ namaḥ
59	ॐ ऐं रौं नमः	oṃ aiṃ rauṃ namaḥ
60	ॐ ऐं स्हौं नमः	oṃ aiṃ shauṃ namaḥ
61	ॐ ऐं कुं नमः	oṃ aiṃ kuṃ namaḥ
62	ॐ ऐं शौं नमः	oṃ aiṃ śauṃ namaḥ

63	ॐ ऐं श्रौं नमः	oṃ aiṃ śrauṃ namaḥ
64	ॐ ऐं वं नमः	oṃ aiṃ vaṃ namaḥ
65	ॐ ऐं त्रूं नमः	oṃ aiṃ trūṃ namaḥ
66	ॐ ऐं क्रौं नमः	oṃ aiṃ krauṃ namaḥ
67	ॐ ऐं क्लं नमः	oṃ aiṃ klaṃ namaḥ
68	ॐ ऐं क्लीं नमः	oṃ aiṃ klīṃ namaḥ
69	ॐ ऐं श्रीं नमः	oṃ aiṃ śrīṃ namaḥ
70	ॐ ऐं ब्लूं नमः	oṃ aiṃ blūṃ namaḥ
71	ॐ ऐं ठां नमः	oṃ aiṃ ṭhāṃ namaḥ
72	ॐ ऐं ह्रीं नमः	oṃ aiṃ hrīṃ namaḥ
73	ॐ ऐं स्त्रां नमः	oṃ aiṃ strāṃ namaḥ
74	ॐ ऐं स्लूं नमः	oṃ aiṃ slūṃ namaḥ
75	ॐ ऐं क्रैं नमः	oṃ aiṃ kraiṃ namaḥ
76	ॐ ऐं त्रां नमः	oṃ aiṃ trāṃ namaḥ
77	ॐ ऐं फ्रां नमः	oṃ aiṃ phrāṃ namaḥ
78	ॐ ऐं जीं नमः	oṃ aiṃ jīṃ namaḥ
79	ॐ ऐं लूं नमः	oṃ aiṃ lūṃ namaḥ
80	ॐ ऐं स्लूं नमः	oṃ aiṃ slūṃ namaḥ
81	ॐ ऐं नों नमः	oṃ aiṃ noṃ namaḥ
82	ॐ ऐं स्त्रीं नमः	oṃ aiṃ strīṃ namaḥ
83	ॐ ऐं प्रूं नमः	oṃ aiṃ prūṃ namaḥ

84	ॐ ऐं सूं नमः	oṃ aiṃ sūṃ namaḥ
85	ॐ ऐं ज्रां नमः	oṃ aiṃ jrāṃ namaḥ
86	ॐ ऐं वौं नमः	oṃ aiṃ vauṃ namaḥ
87	ॐ ऐं ओं नमः	oṃ aiṃ oṃ namaḥ
88	ॐ ऐं श्रौं नमः	oṃ aiṃ śrauṃ namaḥ
89	ॐ ऐं ऋं नमः	oṃ aiṃ ṛṃ namaḥ
90	ॐ ऐं रूं नमः	oṃ aiṃ rūṃ namaḥ
91	ॐ ऐं क्लीं नमः	oṃ aiṃ klīṃ namaḥ
92	ॐ ऐं दुं नमः	oṃ aiṃ duṃ namaḥ
93	ॐ ऐं ह्रीं नमः	oṃ aiṃ hrīṃ namaḥ
94	ॐ ऐं गूं नमः	oṃ aiṃ gūṃ namaḥ
95	ॐ ऐं लां नमः	oṃ aiṃ lāṃ namaḥ
96	ॐ ऐं ह्रां नमः	oṃ aiṃ hrāṃ namaḥ
97	ॐ ऐं गं नमः	oṃ aiṃ gaṃ namaḥ
98	ॐ ऐं ऐं नमः	oṃ aiṃ aiṃ namaḥ
99	ॐ ऐं श्रौं नमः	oṃ aiṃ śrauṃ namaḥ
100	ॐ ऐं जूं नमः	oṃ aiṃ jūṃ namaḥ
101	ॐ ऐं डें नमः	oṃ aiṃ ḍeṃ namaḥ
102	ॐ ऐं श्रौं नमः	oṃ aiṃ śrauṃ namaḥ

103	ॐ ऐं छां नमः	oṃ aiṃ chāṃ namaḥ
104	ॐ ऐं क्लीं नमः	oṃ aiṃ klīṃ namaḥ

ॐ श्रीं क्लीं ह्रीं ह्रीं फट् स्वाहा

oṃ śrīṃ klīṃ hrīṃ hrīṃ phaṭ svāhā

इतिप्रथमोध्यायः

iti prathamodhyāyaḥ

Here ends Chapter One

अथ द्वितीयोऽध्यायः — atha dvitīyo-dhyāyaḥ

1	ॐ ऐं श्रौं नमः	oṃ aiṃ śrauṃ namaḥ
2	ॐ ऐं श्रीं नमः	oṃ aiṃ śrīṃ namaḥ
3	ॐ ऐं ह्सूं नमः	oṃ aiṃ hsūṃ namaḥ
4	ॐ ऐं हौं नमः	oṃ aiṃ hauṃ namaḥ
5	ॐ ऐं ह्रीं नमः	oṃ aiṃ hrīṃ namaḥ
6	ॐ ऐं अं नमः	oṃ aiṃ aṃ namaḥ
7	ॐ ऐं क्लीं नमः	oṃ aiṃ klīṃ namaḥ
8	ॐ ऐं चां नमः	oṃ aiṃ cāṃ namaḥ
9	ॐ ऐं मुं नमः	oṃ aiṃ muṃ namaḥ
10	ॐ ऐं डां नमः	oṃ aiṃ ḍāṃ namaḥ
11	ॐ ऐं यैं नमः	oṃ aiṃ yaiṃ namaḥ
12	ॐ ऐं विं नमः	oṃ aiṃ viṃ namaḥ
13	ॐ ऐं च्चें नमः	oṃ aiṃ cceṃ namaḥ
14	ॐ ऐं ईं नमः	oṃ aiṃ īṃ namaḥ
15	ॐ ऐं सौं नमः	oṃ aiṃ sauṃ namaḥ
16	ॐ ऐं व्रां नमः	oṃ aiṃ vrāṃ namaḥ
17	ॐ ऐं त्रौं नमः	oṃ aiṃ trauṃ namaḥ
18	ॐ ऐं लूं नमः	oṃ aiṃ lūṃ namaḥ
19	ॐ ऐं वं नमः	oṃ aiṃ vaṃ namaḥ
20	ॐ ऐं ह्रां नमः	oṃ aiṃ hrāṃ namaḥ

21	ॐ ऐं क्रीं नमः	oṃ aiṃ krīṃ namaḥ
22	ॐ ऐं सौं नमः	oṃ aiṃ sauṃ namaḥ
23	ॐ ऐं यं नमः	oṃ aiṃ yaṃ namaḥ
24	ॐ ऐं ऐं नमः	oṃ aiṃ aiṃ namaḥ
25	ॐ ऐं मूं नमः	oṃ aiṃ mūṃ namaḥ
26	ॐ ऐं सः नमः	oṃ aiṃ saḥ namaḥ
27	ॐ ऐं हं नमः	oṃ aiṃ haṃ namaḥ
28	ॐ ऐं सं नमः	oṃ aiṃ saṃ namaḥ
29	ॐ ऐं सों नमः	oṃ aiṃ soṃ namaḥ
30	ॐ ऐं शं नमः	oṃ aiṃ śaṃ namaḥ
31	ॐ ऐं हं नमः	oṃ aiṃ haṃ namaḥ
32	ॐ ऐं ह्रौं नमः	oṃ aiṃ hrauṃ namaḥ
33	ॐ ऐं म्लीं नमः	oṃ aiṃ mlīṃ namaḥ
34	ॐ ऐं यूं नमः	oṃ aiṃ yūṃ namaḥ
35	ॐ ऐं त्रूं नमः	oṃ aiṃ trūṃ namaḥ
36	ॐ ऐं स्त्रीं नमः	oṃ aiṃ srīṃ namaḥ
37	ॐ ऐं आं नमः	oṃ aiṃ āṃ namaḥ
38	ॐ ऐं प्रें नमः	oṃ aiṃ preṃ namaḥ
39	ॐ ऐं शं नमः	oṃ aiṃ śaṃ namaḥ
40	ॐ ऐं ह्रां नमः	oṃ aiṃ hrāṃ namaḥ
41	ॐ ऐं स्मूं नमः	oṃ aiṃ smūṃ namaḥ

42	ॐ ऐं ऊं नमः	oṃ aiṃ ūṃ namaḥ
43	ॐ ऐं गूं नमः	oṃ aiṃ gūṃ namaḥ
44	ॐ ऐं व्यं नमः	oṃ aiṃ vyaṃ namaḥ
45	ॐ ऐं ह्रं नमः	oṃ aiṃ hraṃ namaḥ
46	ॐ ऐं भैं नमः	oṃ aiṃ bhaiṃ namaḥ
47	ॐ ऐं ह्रां नमः	oṃ aiṃ hrāṃ namaḥ
48	ॐ ऐं क्रूं नमः	oṃ aiṃ krūṃ namaḥ
49	ॐ ऐं मूं नमः	oṃ aiṃ mūṃ namaḥ
50	ॐ ऐं ल्रीं नमः	oṃ aiṃ lrīṃ namaḥ
51	ॐ ऐं श्रां नमः	oṃ aiṃ śrāṃ namaḥ
52	ॐ ऐं द्रूं नमः	oṃ aiṃ drūṃ namaḥ
53	ॐ ऐं ह्रूं नमः	oṃ aiṃ hrūṃ namaḥ
54	ॐ ऐं ह्सौं नमः	oṃ aiṃ hsauṃ namaḥ
55	ॐ ऐं क्रां नमः	oṃ aiṃ krāṃ namaḥ
56	ॐ ऐं स्हौं नमः	oṃ aiṃ shauṃ namaḥ
57	ॐ ऐं म्लूं नमः	oṃ aiṃ mlūṃ namaḥ
58	ॐ ऐं श्रीं नमः	oṃ aiṃ śrīṃ namaḥ
59	ॐ ऐं गैं नमः	oṃ aiṃ gaiṃ namaḥ
60	ॐ ऐं क्रीं नमः	oṃ aiṃ krīṃ namaḥ
61	ॐ ऐं त्रीं नमः	oṃ aiṃ trīṃ namaḥ
62	ॐ ऐं क्सीं नमः	oṃ aiṃ ksīṃ namaḥ

63	ॐ ऐं फ्रां नमः	oṃ aiṃ phrāṃ namaḥ
64	ॐ ऐं फ्रैं नमः	oṃ aiṃ phraiṃ namaḥ
65	ॐ ऐं ह्रीं नमः	oṃ aiṃ hrīṃ namaḥ
66	ॐ ऐं शां नमः	oṃ aiṃ śāṃ namaḥ
67	ॐ ऐं क्ष्म्रीं नमः	oṃ aiṃ kṣmrīṃ namaḥ
68	ॐ ऐं रौं नमः	oṃ aiṃ rauṃ namaḥ
69	ॐ ऐं ङूं नमः	oṃ aiṃ ṅūṃ namaḥ

ॐ ऐं क्रीं क्रां सौं सः फट् स्वाहा

oṃ aiṃ krīṃ krāṃ sauṃ saḥ phaṭ svāhā

इति द्वितीयोऽध्यायः

iti dvitīyo-dhyāyaḥ

Here ends Chapter Two

अथ तृतीयोऽध्यायः atha tṛtīyo-dhyāyaḥ

1	ॐ ऐं श्रौं नमः	oṃ aiṃ śrauṃ namaḥ
2	ॐ ऐं क्लीं नमः	oṃ aiṃ klīṃ namaḥ
3	ॐ ऐं सां नमः	oṃ aiṃ sāṃ namaḥ
4	ॐ ऐं त्रों नमः	oṃ aiṃ troṃ namaḥ
5	ॐ ऐं प्रूं नमः	oṃ aiṃ prūṃ namaḥ
6	ॐ ऐं ग्लौं नमः	oṃ aiṃ glauṃ namaḥ
7	ॐ ऐं क्रौं नमः	oṃ aiṃ krauṃ namaḥ
8	ॐ ऐं व्रीं नमः	oṃ aiṃ vrīṃ namaḥ
9	ॐ ऐं स्लीं नमः	oṃ aiṃ slīṃ namaḥ
10	ॐ ऐं ह्रीं नमः	oṃ aiṃ hrīṃ namaḥ
11	ॐ ऐं हौं नमः	oṃ aiṃ hauṃ namaḥ
12	ॐ ऐं श्रां नमः	oṃ aiṃ śrāṃ namaḥ
13	ॐ ऐं ग्रीं नमः	oṃ aiṃ grīṃ namaḥ
14	ॐ ऐं क्रूं नमः	oṃ aiṃ krūṃ namaḥ
15	ॐ ऐं क्रीं नमः	oṃ aiṃ krīṃ namaḥ
16	ॐ ऐं यां नमः	oṃ aiṃ yāṃ namaḥ
17	ॐ ऐं द्लूं नमः	oṃ aiṃ dlūṃ namaḥ
18	ॐ ऐं द्रूं नमः	oṃ aiṃ drūṃ namaḥ
19	ॐ ऐं क्षं नमः	oṃ aiṃ kṣaṃ namaḥ
20	ॐ ऐं ओं नमः	oṃ aiṃ oṃ namaḥ

21	ॐ ऐं क्रौं नमः	oṃ aiṃ krauṃ namaḥ
22	ॐ ऐं क्ष्म्क्ल्रीं नमः	oṃ aiṃ kṣmklrīṃ namaḥ
23	ॐ ऐं वां नमः	oṃ aiṃ vāṃ namaḥ
24	ॐ ऐं श्रूं नमः	oṃ aiṃ śrūṃ namaḥ
25	ॐ ऐं ग्लूं नमः	oṃ aiṃ glūṃ namaḥ
26	ॐ ऐं ल्रीं नमः	oṃ aiṃ lrīṃ namaḥ
27	ॐ ऐं प्रें नमः	oṃ aiṃ preṃ namaḥ
28	ॐ ऐं हूं नमः	oṃ aiṃ hūṃ namaḥ
29	ॐ ऐं ह्रौं नमः	oṃ aiṃ hrauṃ namaḥ
30	ॐ ऐं दें नमः	oṃ aiṃ deṃ namaḥ
31	ॐ ऐं नूं नमः	oṃ aiṃ nūṃ namaḥ
32	ॐ ऐं आं नमः	oṃ aiṃ āṃ namaḥ
33	ॐ ऐं फ्रां नमः	oṃ aiṃ phrāṃ namaḥ
34	ॐ ऐं प्रीं नमः	oṃ aiṃ prīṃ namaḥ
35	ॐ ऐं दं नमः	oṃ aiṃ daṃ namaḥ
36	ॐ ऐं फ्रीं नमः	oṃ aiṃ phrīṃ namaḥ
37	ॐ ऐं ह्रीं नमः	oṃ aiṃ hrīṃ namaḥ
38	ॐ ऐं गूं नमः	oṃ aiṃ gūṃ namaḥ
39	ॐ ऐं श्रौं नमः	oṃ aiṃ śrauṃ namaḥ
40	ॐ ऐं सां नमः	oṃ aiṃ sāṃ namaḥ
41	ॐ ऐं श्रीं नमः	oṃ aiṃ śrīṃ namaḥ

42	ॐ ऐं जुं नमः	oṃ aiṃ juṃ namaḥ
43	ॐ ऐं हं नमः	oṃ aiṃ haṃ namaḥ
44	ॐ ऐं सं नमः	oṃ aiṃ saṃ namaḥ

ॐ ह्रीं श्रीं कुं फट् स्वाहा
oṃ hrīṃ śrīṃ kuṃ phaṭ svāhā

इतितृतीयोऽध्यायः
iti tṛtīyo-dhyāyaḥ
Here ends Chapter Three

अथ चतुर्थोऽध्यायः atha caturtho-dhyāyaḥ

1	ॐ ऐं श्रौं नमः	oṃ aiṃ śrauṃ namaḥ
2	ॐ ऐं सौं नमः	oṃ aiṃ sauṃ namaḥ
3	ॐ ऐं दीं नमः	oṃ aiṃ dīṃ namaḥ
4	ॐ ऐं प्रें नमः	oṃ aiṃ preṃ namaḥ
5	ॐ ऐं यां नमः	oṃ aiṃ yāṃ namaḥ
6	ॐ ऐं रूं नमः	oṃ aiṃ rūṃ namaḥ
7	ॐ ऐं मं नमः	oṃ aiṃ maṃ namaḥ
8	ॐ ऐं सूं नमः	oṃ aiṃ sūṃ namaḥ
9	ॐ ऐं श्रां नमः	oṃ aiṃ śrāṃ namaḥ
10	ॐ ऐं औं नमः	oṃ aiṃ auṃ namaḥ
11	ॐ ऐं लूं नमः	oṃ aiṃ lūṃ namaḥ
12	ॐ ऐं डूं नमः	oṃ aiṃ ḍūṃ namaḥ
13	ॐ ऐं जूं नमः	oṃ aiṃ jūṃ namaḥ
14	ॐ ऐं धूं नमः	oṃ aiṃ dhūṃ namaḥ
15	ॐ ऐं त्रें नमः	oṃ aiṃ treṃ namaḥ
16	ॐ ऐं ह्रीं नमः	oṃ aiṃ hrīṃ namaḥ
17	ॐ ऐं श्रीं नमः	oṃ aiṃ śrīṃ namaḥ
18	ॐ ऐं ईं नमः	oṃ aiṃ īṃ namaḥ
19	ॐ ऐं ह्रां नमः	oṃ aiṃ hrāṃ namaḥ
20	ॐ ऐं ह्लूं नमः	oṃ aiṃ hlrūṃ namaḥ

21	ॐ ऐं क्लूं नमः	oṃ aiṃ klūṃ namaḥ
22	ॐ ऐं क्रां नमः	oṃ aiṃ krāṃ namaḥ
23	ॐ ऐं ल्लूं नमः	oṃ aiṃ llūṃ namaḥ
24	ॐ ऐं फ्रें नमः	oṃ aiṃ phreṃ namaḥ
25	ॐ ऐं क्रीं नमः	oṃ aiṃ krīṃ namaḥ
26	ॐ ऐं म्लूं नमः	oṃ aiṃ mlūṃ namaḥ
27	ॐ ऐं घ्रें नमः	oṃ aiṃ ghreṃ namaḥ
28	ॐ ऐं श्रौं नमः	oṃ aiṃ śrauṃ namaḥ
29	ॐ ऐं ह्रौं नमः	oṃ aiṃ hrauṃ namaḥ
30	ॐ ऐं व्रीं नमः	oṃ aiṃ vrīṃ namaḥ
31	ॐ ऐं ह्रीं नमः	oṃ aiṃ hrīṃ namaḥ
32	ॐ ऐं त्रौं नमः	oṃ aiṃ trauṃ namaḥ
33	ॐ ऐं ह्लौं नमः	oṃ aiṃ hllauṃ namaḥ
34	ॐ ऐं गीं नमः	oṃ aiṃ gīṃ namaḥ
35	ॐ ऐं यूं नमः	oṃ aiṃ yūṃ namaḥ
36	ॐ ऐं ह्लीं नमः	oṃ aiṃ hlīṃ namaḥ
37	ॐ ऐं ह्लूं नमः	oṃ aiṃ hlūṃ namaḥ
38	ॐ ऐं श्रौं नमः	oṃ aiṃ śrauṃ namaḥ
39	ॐ ऐं ओं नमः	oṃ aiṃ oṃ namaḥ
40	ॐ ऐं अं नमः	oṃ aiṃ aṃ namaḥ

41	ॐ ऐं म्हौं नमः	oṃ aiṃ mhauṃ namaḥ
42	ॐ ऐं प्रीं नमः	oṃ aiṃ prīṃ namaḥ

ॐ अं ह्रीं श्रीं हंसः फट् स्वाहा

oṃ aṃ hrīṃ śrīṃ haṃsaḥ phaṭ svāhā

इति चतुर्थोऽध्यायः

iti caturtho-dhyāyaḥ

Here ends Chapter Four

अथ पञ्चमोऽध्यायः — atha pañcamo-dhyāyaḥ

1	ॐ ऐं श्रौं नमः	oṃ aiṃ śrauṃ namaḥ
2	ॐ ऐं प्रीं नमः	oṃ aiṃ prīṃ namaḥ
3	ॐ ऐं ओं नमः	oṃ aiṃ oṃ namaḥ
4	ॐ ऐं ह्रीं नमः	oṃ aiṃ hrīṃ namaḥ
5	ॐ ऐं ल्रीं नमः	oṃ aiṃ lrīṃ namaḥ
6	ॐ ऐं त्रों नमः	oṃ aiṃ troṃ namaḥ
7	ॐ ऐं क्रीं नमः	oṃ aiṃ krīṃ namaḥ
8	ॐ ऐं ह्सौं नमः	oṃ aiṃ hsauṃ namaḥ
9	ॐ ऐं ह्रीं नमः	oṃ aiṃ hrīṃ namaḥ
10	ॐ ऐं श्रीं नमः	oṃ aiṃ śrīṃ namaḥ
11	ॐ ऐं हूं नमः	oṃ aiṃ hūṃ namaḥ
12	ॐ ऐं क्लीं नमः	oṃ aiṃ klīṃ namaḥ
13	ॐ ऐं रौं नमः	oṃ aiṃ rauṃ namaḥ
14	ॐ ऐं स्त्रीं नमः	oṃ aiṃ strīṃ namaḥ
15	ॐ ऐं म्लीं नमः	oṃ aiṃ mlīṃ namaḥ
16	ॐ ऐं प्लूं नमः	oṃ aiṃ plūṃ namaḥ
17	ॐ ऐं स्हौं नमः	oṃ aiṃ shauṃ namaḥ
18	ॐ ऐं स्त्रीं नमः	oṃ aiṃ strīṃ namaḥ
19	ॐ ऐं ग्लूं नमः	oṃ aiṃ glūṃ namaḥ
20	ॐ ऐं व्रीं नमः	oṃ aiṃ vrīṃ namaḥ

21	ॐ ऐं सौं नमः	oṃ aiṃ sauṃ namaḥ
22	ॐ ऐं लूं नमः	oṃ aiṃ lūṃ namaḥ
23	ॐ ऐं ल्लूं नमः	oṃ aiṃ llūṃ namaḥ
24	ॐ ऐं द्रां नमः	oṃ aiṃ drāṃ namaḥ
25	ॐ ऐं क्सां नमः	oṃ aiṃ ksāṃ namaḥ
26	ॐ ऐं क्ष्म्रीं नमः	oṃ aiṃ kṣmrīṃ namaḥ
27	ॐ ऐं ग्लौं नमः	oṃ aiṃ glauṃ namaḥ
28	ॐ ऐं स्कं नमः	oṃ aiṃ skaṃ namaḥ
29	ॐ ऐं बूं नमः	oṃ aiṃ būṃ namaḥ
30	ॐ ऐं स्क्लूं नमः	oṃ aiṃ sklūṃ namaḥ
31	ॐ ऐं क्रौं नमः	oṃ aiṃ krauṃ namaḥ
32	ॐ ऐं छ्रीं नमः	oṃ aiṃ chrīṃ namaḥ
33	ॐ ऐं म्लूं नमः	oṃ aiṃ mlūṃ namaḥ
34	ॐ ऐं क्लूं नमः	oṃ aiṃ klūṃ namaḥ
35	ॐ ऐं शां नमः	oṃ aiṃ śāṃ namaḥ
36	ॐ ऐं ल्हीं नमः	oṃ aiṃ lhīṃ namaḥ
37	ॐ ऐं स्रूं नमः	oṃ aiṃ srūṃ namaḥ
38	ॐ ऐं ल्लीं नमः	oṃ aiṃ llīṃ namaḥ
39	ॐ ऐं लीं नमः	oṃ aiṃ līṃ namaḥ
40	ॐ ऐं सं नमः	oṃ aiṃ saṃ namaḥ
41	ॐ ऐं लूं नमः	oṃ aiṃ lūṃ namaḥ

42	ॐ ऐं ह्सूं नमः	oṃ aiṃ hsūṃ namaḥ
43	ॐ ऐं श्रूं नमः	oṃ aiṃ śrūṃ namaḥ
44	ॐ ऐं जूं नमः	oṃ aiṃ jūṃ namaḥ
45	ॐ ऐं ह्स्लीं नमः	oṃ aiṃ hslrīṃ namaḥ
46	ॐ ऐं स्कीं नमः	oṃ aiṃ skīṃ namaḥ
47	ॐ ऐं क्लां नमः	oṃ aiṃ klāṃ namaḥ
48	ॐ ऐं श्रूं नमः	oṃ aiṃ śrūṃ namaḥ
49	ॐ ऐं हं नमः	oṃ aiṃ haṃ namaḥ
50	ॐ ऐं ह्लीं नमः	oṃ aiṃ hlīṃ namaḥ
51	ॐ ऐं क्स्रूं नमः	oṃ aiṃ ksrūṃ namaḥ
52	ॐ ऐं द्रौं नमः	oṃ aiṃ drauṃ namaḥ
53	ॐ ऐं क्लूं नमः	oṃ aiṃ klūṃ namaḥ
54	ॐ ऐं गां नमः	oṃ aiṃ gāṃ namaḥ
55	ॐ ऐं सं नमः	oṃ aiṃ saṃ namaḥ
56	ॐ ऐं ल्स्रां नमः	oṃ aiṃ lsrāṃ namaḥ
57	ॐ ऐं फ्रीं नमः	oṃ aiṃ phrīṃ namaḥ
58	ॐ ऐं स्लां नमः	oṃ aiṃ slāṃ namaḥ
59	ॐ ऐं ल्लूं नमः	oṃ aiṃ llūṃ namaḥ
60	ॐ ऐं फ्रें नमः	oṃ aiṃ phreṃ namaḥ
61	ॐ ऐं ओं नमः	oṃ aiṃ oṃ namaḥ
62	ॐ ऐं स्म्लीं नमः	oṃ aiṃ smlīṃ namaḥ

63	ॐ ऐं ह्रां नमः	oṃ aiṃ hrāṃ namaḥ
64	ॐ ऐं ॐ नमः	oṃ aiṃ oṃ namaḥ
65	ॐ ऐं ह्लूं नमः	oṃ aiṃ hlūṃ namaḥ
66	ॐ ऐं हूं नमः	oṃ aiṃ hūṃ namaḥ
67	ॐ ऐं नं नमः	oṃ aiṃ naṃ namaḥ
68	ॐ ऐं स्रां नमः	oṃ aiṃ srāṃ namaḥ
69	ॐ ऐं वं नमः	oṃ aiṃ vaṃ namaḥ
70	ॐ ऐं मं नमः	oṃ aiṃ maṃ namaḥ
71	ॐ ऐं म्व्लीं नमः	oṃ aiṃ mvlīṃ namaḥ
72	ॐ ऐं शां नमः	oṃ aiṃ śāṃ namaḥ
73	ॐ ऐं लं नमः	oṃ aiṃ laṃ namaḥ
74	ॐ ऐं भैं नमः	oṃ aiṃ bhaiṃ namaḥ
75	ॐ ऐं ल्लूं नमः	oṃ aiṃ llūṃ namaḥ
76	ॐ ऐं हौं नमः	oṃ aiṃ hauṃ namaḥ
77	ॐ ऐं ईं नमः	oṃ aiṃ īṃ namaḥ oṃ
78	ॐ ऐं चें नमः	aiṃ ceṃ namaḥ oṃ
79	ॐ ऐं ल्क्रीं नमः	aiṃ lkrīṃ namaḥ oṃ
80	ॐ ऐं ह्ल्रीं नमः	aiṃ hlrīṃ namaḥ oṃ
81	ॐ ऐं क्ष्म्ल्रीं नमः	aiṃ kṣmlrīṃ namaḥ
82	ॐ ऐं पूं नमः	oṃ aiṃ pūṃ namaḥ
83	ॐ ऐं श्रौं नमः	oṃ aiṃ śrauṃ namaḥ

84	ॐ ऐं ह्रौं नमः	oṃ aiṃ hrauṃ namaḥ
85	ॐ ऐं भ्रूं नमः	oṃ aiṃ bhrūṃ namaḥ
86	ॐ ऐं क्स्त्रीं नमः	oṃ aiṃ kstrīṃ namaḥ
87	ॐ ऐं आं नमः	oṃ aiṃ āṃ namaḥ
88	ॐ ऐं क्रूं नमः	oṃ aiṃ krūṃ namaḥ
89	ॐ ऐं त्रूं नमः	oṃ aiṃ trūṃ namaḥ
90	ॐ ऐं डुं नमः	oṃ aiṃ ḍuṃ namaḥ
91	ॐ ऐं जां नमः	oṃ aiṃ jāṃ namaḥ
92	ॐ ऐं ह्लृूं नमः	oṃ aiṃ hlrūṃ namaḥ
93	ॐ ऐं फ्रौं नमः	oṃ aiṃ phrauṃ namaḥ
94	ॐ ऐं क्रौं नमः	oṃ aiṃ krauṃ namaḥ
95	ॐ ऐं किं नमः	oṃ aiṃ kiṃ namaḥ
96	ॐ ऐं ग्लूं नमः	oṃ aiṃ glūṃ namaḥ
97	ॐ ऐं छ्र्क्लीं नमः	oṃ aiṃ chrklīṃ namaḥ
98	ॐ ऐं रं नमः	oṃ aiṃ raṃ namaḥ
99	ॐ ऐं क्सैं नमः	oṃ aiṃ ksaiṃ namaḥ
100	ॐ ऐं स्हुं नमः	oṃ aiṃ shuṃ namaḥ
101	ॐ ऐं श्रौं नमः	oṃ aiṃ śrauṃ namaḥ
102	ॐ ऐं श्श्रीं नमः	oṃ aiṃ śrśrīṃ namaḥ
103	ॐ ऐं ओं नमः	oṃ aiṃ oṃ namaḥ
104	ॐ ऐं लूं नमः	oṃ aiṃ lūṃ namaḥ

105	ॐ ऐं ल्हूं नमः	oṃ aiṃ lhūṃ namaḥ
106	ॐ ऐं ल्लूं नमः	oṃ aiṃ llūṃ namaḥ
107	ॐ ऐं स्क्रीं नमः	oṃ aiṃ skrīṃ namaḥ
108	ॐ ऐं स्स्त्रौं नमः	oṃ aiṃ sstrauṃ namaḥ
109	ॐ ऐं स्भ्रूं नमः	oṃ aiṃ sbhrūṃ namaḥ
110	ॐ ऐं क्ष्म्क्लीं नमः	oṃ aiṃ kṣmklīṃ namaḥ
111	ॐ ऐं व्रीं नमः	oṃ aiṃ vrīṃ namaḥ
112	ॐ ऐं सीं नमः	oṃ aiṃ sīṃ namaḥ
113	ॐ ऐं भूं नमः	oṃ aiṃ bhūṃ namaḥ
114	ॐ ऐं लां नमः	oṃ aiṃ lāṃ namaḥ
115	ॐ ऐं श्रौं नमः	oṃ aiṃ śrauṃ namaḥ
116	ॐ ऐं स्हैं नमः	oṃ aiṃ shaiṃ namaḥ
117	ॐ ऐं ह्रीं नमः	oṃ aiṃ hrīṃ namaḥ
118	ॐ ऐं श्रीं नमः	oṃ aiṃ śrīṃ namaḥ
119	ॐ ऐं फ्रें नमः	oṃ aiṃ phreṃ namaḥ
120	ॐ ऐं रूं नमः	oṃ aiṃ rūṃ namaḥ
121	ॐ ऐं च्छ्रूं नमः	oṃ aiṃ cchrūṃ namaḥ
122	ॐ ऐं ल्हूं नमः	oṃ aiṃ lhūṃ namaḥ
123	ॐ ऐं कं नमः	oṃ aiṃ kaṃ namaḥ
124	ॐ ऐं द्रें नमः	oṃ aiṃ dreṃ namaḥ
125	ॐ ऐं श्रीं नमः	oṃ aiṃ śrīṃ namaḥ

126	ॐ ऐं सां नमः	oṃ aiṃ sāṃ namaḥ
127	ॐ ऐं ह्रीं नमः	oṃ aiṃ hrīṃ namaḥ
128	ॐ ऐं ऐं नमः	oṃ aiṃ aiṃ namaḥ
129	ॐ ऐं स्क्लीं नमः	oṃ aiṃ sklīṃ namaḥ

ओं ऐं ह्रीं क्लीं चामुण्डायै विच्चे स्वाहा
oṃ aiṃ hrīṃ klīṃ cāmuṇḍāyai vicce svāhā

इतिपञ्चमोऽध्यायः
iti pañcamo-dhyāyaḥ
Here ends Chapter Five

अथ षष्ठोऽध्यायः atha ṣaṣṭho-dhyāyaḥ

1	ॐ ऐं श्रौं नमः	oṃ aiṃ śrauṃ namaḥ
2	ॐ ऐं ओं नमः	oṃ aiṃ oṃ namaḥ
3	ॐ ऐं त्रूं नमः	oṃ aiṃ trūṃ namaḥ
4	ॐ ऐं ह्रौं नमः	oṃ aiṃ hrauṃ namaḥ
5	ॐ ऐं क्रौं नमः	oṃ aiṃ krauṃ namaḥ
6	ॐ ऐं ह्रीं नमः	oṃ aiṃ hrīṃ namaḥ
7	ॐ ऐं त्रीं नमः	oṃ aiṃ trīṃ namaḥ
8	ॐ ऐं क्लीं नमः	oṃ aiṃ klīṃ namaḥ
9	ॐ ऐं प्रीं नमः	oṃ aiṃ prīṃ namaḥ
10	ॐ ऐं ह्रीं नमः	oṃ aiṃ hrīṃ namaḥ
11	ॐ ऐं ह्रौं नमः	oṃ aiṃ hrauṃ namaḥ
12	ॐ ऐं श्रौं नमः	oṃ aiṃ śrauṃ namaḥ
13	ॐ ऐं ऐं नमः	oṃ aiṃ aiṃ namaḥ
14	ॐ ऐं ओं नमः	oṃ aiṃ oṃ namaḥ
15	ॐ ऐं श्रीं नमः	oṃ aiṃ śrīṃ namaḥ
16	ॐ ऐं क्रां नमः	oṃ aiṃ krāṃ namaḥ
17	ॐ ऐं हूं नमः	oṃ aiṃ hūṃ namaḥ
18	ॐ ऐं छ्रां नमः	oṃ aiṃ chrāṃ namaḥ
19	ॐ ऐं क्ष्म्क्ल्रीं नमः	oṃ aiṃ kṣmklrīṃ namaḥ
20	ॐ ऐं ल्लूं नमः	oṃ aiṃ llūṃ namaḥ

21 ॐ ऐं सौं नमः oṃ aiṃ sauṃ namaḥ

22 ॐ ऐं ह्लौं नमः oṃ aiṃ hlauṃ namaḥ

23 ॐ ऐं क्रूं नमः oṃ aiṃ krūṃ namaḥ

24 ॐ ऐं सौं नमः oṃ aiṃ sauṃ namaḥ

ॐ श्रीं यं ह्रीं क्लीं ह्रीं फट् स्वाहा

oṃ śrīṃ yaṃ hrīṃ klīṃ hrīṃ phaṭ svāhā

इतिषष्ठोऽध्यायः

iti ṣaṣṭho-dhyāyaḥ

Here ends Chapter Six

अथ सप्तमोऽध्यायः   atha saptamo-dhyāyaḥ

1	ॐ ऐं श्रौं नमः	oṃ aiṃ śrauṃ namaḥ
2	ॐ ऐं कूं नमः	oṃ aiṃ kūṃ namaḥ
3	ॐ ऐं ह्लीं नमः	oṃ aiṃ hlīṃ namaḥ
4	ॐ ऐं ह्रं नमः	oṃ aiṃ hraṃ namaḥ
5	ॐ ऐं मूं नमः	oṃ aiṃ mūṃ namaḥ
6	ॐ ऐं त्रौं नमः	oṃ aiṃ trauṃ namaḥ
7	ॐ ऐं ह्रौं नमः	oṃ aiṃ hrauṃ namaḥ
8	ॐ ऐं ओं नमः	oṃ aiṃ oṃ namaḥ
9	ॐ ऐं ह्सूं नमः	oṃ aiṃ hsūṃ namaḥ
10	ॐ ऐं क्लूं नमः	oṃ aiṃ klūṃ namaḥ
11	ॐ ऐं क्रें नमः	oṃ aiṃ kreṃ namaḥ
12	ॐ ऐं नें नमः	oṃ aiṃ neṃ namaḥ
13	ॐ ऐं लूं नमः	oṃ aiṃ lūṃ namaḥ
14	ॐ ऐं ह्स्लीं नमः	oṃ aiṃ hslīṃ namaḥ
15	ॐ ऐं प्लूं नमः	oṃ aiṃ plūṃ namaḥ
16	ॐ ऐं शां नमः	oṃ aiṃ śāṃ namaḥ
17	ॐ ऐं स्लूं नमः	oṃ aiṃ slūṃ namaḥ
18	ॐ ऐं प्लीं नमः	oṃ aiṃ plīṃ namaḥ
19	ॐ ऐं प्रें नमः	oṃ aiṃ preṃ namaḥ
20	ॐ ऐं अं नमः	oṃ aiṃ aṃ namaḥ

21	ॐ ऐं औं नमः	oṃ aiṃ auṃ namaḥ
22	ॐ ऐं म्लृीं नमः	oṃ aiṃ mlrīṃ namaḥ
23	ॐ ऐं श्रां नमः	oṃ aiṃ śrāṃ namaḥ
24	ॐ ऐं सौं नमः	oṃ aiṃ sauṃ namaḥ
25	ॐ ऐं श्रौं नमः	oṃ aiṃ śrauṃ namaḥ
26	ॐ ऐं प्रीं नमः	oṃ aiṃ prīṃ namaḥ
27	ॐ ऐं ह्स्व्रीं नमः	oṃ aiṃ hsvrīṃ namaḥ

ॐ रं रं रं कं कं कं जं जं जं चामुण्डायै फट् स्वाहा

oṃ raṃ raṃ raṃ kaṃ kaṃ kaṃ jaṃ jaṃ jaṃ cāmuṇḍāyai phaṭ svāhā

इतिसप्तमोऽध्यायः

iti saptamo-dhyāyaḥ

Here ends Chapter Seven

## अथाष्टमोऽध्यायः	atha aṣṭamo-dhyāyaḥ

1	ॐ ऐं श्रौं नमः	oṃ aiṃ śrauṃ namaḥ
2	ॐ ऐं म्ह्ल्रीं नमः	oṃ aiṃ mhlrīṃ namaḥ
3	ॐ ऐं प्रूं नमः	oṃ aiṃ prūṃ namaḥ
4	ॐ ऐं ऐं नमः	oṃ aiṃ aiṃ namaḥ
5	ॐ ऐं क्रों नमः	oṃ aiṃ kroṃ namaḥ
6	ॐ ऐं ईं नमः	oṃ aiṃ īṃ namaḥ
7	ॐ ऐं ऐं नमः	oṃ aiṃ aiṃ namaḥ
8	ॐ ऐं ल्रीं नमः	oṃ aiṃ lrīṃ namaḥ
9	ॐ ऐं फ्रौं नमः	oṃ aiṃ phrauṃ namaḥ
10	ॐ ऐं म्लूं नमः	oṃ aiṃ mlūṃ namaḥ
11	ॐ ऐं नों नमः	oṃ aiṃ noṃ namaḥ
12	ॐ ऐं हूं नमः	oṃ aiṃ hūṃ namaḥ
13	ॐ ऐं फ्रौं नमः	oṃ aiṃ phrauṃ namaḥ
14	ॐ ऐं ग्लौं नमः	oṃ aiṃ glauṃ namaḥ
15	ॐ ऐं स्मौं नमः	oṃ aiṃ smauṃ namaḥ
16	ॐ ऐं सौं नमः	oṃ aiṃ sauṃ namaḥ
17	ॐ ऐं श्रीं नमः	oṃ aiṃ śrīṃ namaḥ
18	ॐ ऐं स्हौं नमः	oṃ aiṃ shauṃ namaḥ
19	ॐ ऐं ख्सें नमः	oṃ aiṃ khseṃ namaḥ
20	ॐ ऐं क्ष्म्लीं नमः	oṃ aiṃ kṣmlīṃ namaḥ

21	ॐ ऐं ह्रां नमः	oṃ aiṃ hrāṃ namaḥ
22	ॐ ऐं वीं नमः	oṃ aiṃ vīṃ namaḥ
23	ॐ ऐं लूं नमः	oṃ aiṃ lūṃ namaḥ
24	ॐ ऐं ल्सीं नमः	oṃ aiṃ lsīṃ namaḥ
25	ॐ ऐं ब्लीं नमः	oṃ aiṃ blīṃ namaḥ
26	ॐ ऐं त्स्रों नमः	oṃ aiṃ tsroṃ namaḥ
27	ॐ ऐं व्रूं नमः	oṃ aiṃ vrūṃ namaḥ
28	ॐ ऐं श्ल्कीं नमः	oṃ aiṃ ślkīṃ namaḥ
29	ॐ ऐं श्रूं नमः	oṃ aiṃ śrūṃ namaḥ
30	ॐ ऐं ह्रीं नमः	oṃ aiṃ hrīṃ namaḥ
31	ॐ ऐं शीं नमः	oṃ aiṃ śīṃ namaḥ
32	ॐ ऐं क्लीं नमः	oṃ aiṃ klīṃ namaḥ
33	ॐ ऐं क्लौं नमः	oṃ aiṃ klauṃ namaḥ
34	ॐ ऐं तीं नमः	oṃ aiṃ tīṃ namaḥ
35	ॐ ऐं ह्रूं नमः	oṃ aiṃ hrūṃ namaḥ
36	ॐ ऐं क्लूं नमः	oṃ aiṃ klūṃ namaḥ
37	ॐ ऐं तां नमः	oṃ aiṃ tāṃ namaḥ
38	ॐ ऐं म्लूं नमः	oṃ aiṃ mlūṃ namaḥ
39	ॐ ऐं हं नमः	oṃ aiṃ haṃ namaḥ
40	ॐ ऐं स्लूं नमः	oṃ aiṃ slūṃ namaḥ
41	ॐ ऐं औं नमः	oṃ aiṃ auṃ namaḥ

42	ॐ ऐं ल्हों नमः	oṃ aiṃ lhoṃ namaḥ
43	ॐ ऐं श्ल्रीं नमः	oṃ aiṃ ślrīṃ namaḥ
44	ॐ ऐं यां नमः	oṃ aiṃ yāṃ namaḥ
45	ॐ ऐं थ्लीं नमः	oṃ aiṃ thlīṃ namaḥ
46	ॐ ऐं ल्हों नमः	oṃ aiṃ lhoṃ namaḥ
47	ॐ ऐं ग्लौं नमः	oṃ aiṃ glauṃ namaḥ
48	ॐ ऐं ह्रौं नमः	oṃ aiṃ hrauṃ namaḥ
49	ॐ ऐं प्रां नमः	oṃ aiṃ prāṃ namaḥ
50	ॐ ऐं क्रीं नमः	oṃ aiṃ krīṃ namaḥ
51	ॐ ऐं क्लीं नमः	oṃ aiṃ klīṃ namaḥ
52	ॐ ऐं न्स्लुं नमः	oṃ aiṃ nsluṃ namaḥ
53	ॐ ऐं हीं नमः	oṃ aiṃ hīṃ namaḥ
54	ॐ ऐं ह्लौं नमः	oṃ aiṃ hlauṃ namaḥ
55	ॐ ऐं ह्रैं नमः	oṃ aiṃ hraiṃ namaḥ
56	ॐ ऐं भ्रं नमः	oṃ aiṃ bhraṃ namaḥ
57	ॐ ऐं सौं नमः	oṃ aiṃ sauṃ namaḥ
58	ॐ ऐं श्रीं नमः	oṃ aiṃ śrīṃ namaḥ
59	ॐ ऐं प्सूं नमः	oṃ aiṃ psūṃ namaḥ
60	ॐ ऐं द्रौं नमः	oṃ aiṃ drauṃ namaḥ
61	ॐ ऐं स्स्रां नमः	oṃ aiṃ ssrāṃ namaḥ

62	ॐ ऐं ह्स्लीं नमः	oṃ aiṃ hslīṃ namaḥ
63	ॐ ऐं स्ल्लीं नमः	oṃ aiṃ sllrīṃ namaḥ

ॐ शां सं श्रीं श्रं अं अः क्लीं हीं फट् स्वाहा

oṃ śāṃ saṃ śrīṃ śraṃ aṃ aḥ klīṃ hīṃ phaṭ svāhā

इत्यष्टमोऽध्यायः

ityaṣṭamo-dhyāyaḥ

Here ends Chapter Eight

अथ नवमोऽध्यायः atha navamo-dhyāyaḥ

1	ॐ ऐं रौं नमः	oṃ aiṃ rauṃ namaḥ
2	ॐ ऐं क्लीं नमः	oṃ aiṃ klīṃ namaḥ
3	ॐ ऐं म्लौं नमः	oṃ aiṃ mlauṃ namaḥ
4	ॐ ऐं श्रौं नमः	oṃ aiṃ śrauṃ namaḥ
5	ॐ ऐं ग्लीं नमः	oṃ aiṃ glīṃ namaḥ
6	ॐ ऐं ह्रौं नमः	oṃ aiṃ hrauṃ namaḥ
7	ॐ ऐं ह्सौं नमः	oṃ aiṃ hsauṃ namaḥ
8	ॐ ऐं ईं नमः	oṃ aiṃ īṃ namaḥ
9	ॐ ऐं व्रूं नमः	oṃ aiṃ vrūṃ namaḥ
10	ॐ ऐं श्रां नमः	oṃ aiṃ śrāṃ namaḥ
11	ॐ ऐं लूं नमः	oṃ aiṃ lūṃ namaḥ
12	ॐ ऐं आं नमः	oṃ aiṃ āṃ namaḥ
13	ॐ ऐं श्रीं नमः	oṃ aiṃ śrīṃ namaḥ
14	ॐ ऐं क्रौं नमः	oṃ aiṃ krauṃ namaḥ
15	ॐ ऐं प्रूं नमः	oṃ aiṃ prūṃ namaḥ
16	ॐ ऐं क्लीं नमः	oṃ aiṃ klīṃ namaḥ
17	ॐ ऐं भ्रूं नमः	oṃ aiṃ bhrūṃ namaḥ
18	ॐ ऐं ह्रौं नमः	oṃ aiṃ hrauṃ namaḥ
19	ॐ ऐं क्रीं नमः	oṃ aiṃ krīṃ namaḥ
20	ॐ ऐं म्लीं नमः	oṃ aiṃ mlīṃ namaḥ

21	ॐ ऐं ग्लौं नमः	oṃ aiṃ glauṃ namaḥ
22	ॐ ऐं ह्सूं नमः	oṃ aiṃ hsūṃ namaḥ
23	ॐ ऐं ल्पीं नमः	oṃ aiṃ lpīṃ namaḥ
24	ॐ ऐं ह्रौं नमः	oṃ aiṃ hrauṃ namaḥ
25	ॐ ऐं ह्स्रां नमः	oṃ aiṃ hsrāṃ namaḥ
26	ॐ ऐं स्हौं नमः	oṃ aiṃ shauṃ namaḥ
27	ॐ ऐं ल्लूं नमः	oṃ aiṃ llūṃ namaḥ
28	ॐ ऐं क्स्लीं नमः	oṃ aiṃ kslīṃ namaḥ
29	ॐ ऐं श्रीं नमः	oṃ aiṃ śrīṃ namaḥ
30	ॐ ऐं स्तूं नमः	oṃ aiṃ stūṃ namaḥ
31	ॐ ऐं च्रें नमः	oṃ aiṃ creṃ namaḥ
32	ॐ ऐं वीं नमः	oṃ aiṃ vīṃ namaḥ
33	ॐ ऐं क्ष्लूं नमः	oṃ aiṃ kṣlūṃ namaḥ
34	ॐ ऐं श्लूं नमः	oṃ aiṃ ślūṃ namaḥ
35	ॐ ऐं क्रूं नमः	oṃ aiṃ krūṃ namaḥ
36	ॐ ऐं क्रां नमः	oṃ aiṃ krāṃ namaḥ
37	ॐ ऐं ह्रौं नमः	oṃ aiṃ hrauṃ namaḥ
38	ॐ ऐं क्रां नमः	oṃ aiṃ krāṃ namaḥ
39	ॐ ऐं स्क्ष्लीं नमः	oṃ aiṃ skṣlīṃ namaḥ

40	ॐ ऐं सूं नमः	oṃ aiṃ sūṃ namaḥ
41	ॐ ऐं फ्रूं नमः	oṃ aiṃ phrūṃ namaḥ

ॐ ऐं ह्रीं श्रीं सौं फट् स्वाहा

oṃ aiṃ hrīṃ śrīṃ sauṃ phaṭ svāhā

इति नवमोऽध्यायः

iti navamo-dhyāyaḥ

Here ends Chapter Nine

अथ दशमोऽध्यायः atha daśamo-dhyāyaḥ

1	ॐ ऐं श्रौं नमः	oṃ aiṃ śrauṃ namaḥ
2	ॐ ऐं ह्रीं नमः	oṃ aiṃ hrīṃ namaḥ
3	ॐ ऐं ब्लूं नमः	oṃ aiṃ blūṃ namaḥ
4	ॐ ऐं ह्रीं नमः	oṃ aiṃ hrīṃ namaḥ
5	ॐ ऐं म्लूं नमः	oṃ aiṃ mlūṃ namaḥ
6	ॐ ऐं श्रौं नमः	oṃ aiṃ śrauṃ namaḥ
7	ॐ ऐं ह्रीं नमः	oṃ aiṃ hrīṃ namaḥ
8	ॐ ऐं ग्लीं नमः	oṃ aiṃ glīṃ namaḥ
9	ॐ ऐं श्रौं नमः	oṃ aiṃ śrauṃ namaḥ
10	ॐ ऐं ध्रूं नमः	oṃ aiṃ dhrūṃ namaḥ
11	ॐ ऐं हुं नमः	oṃ aiṃ huṃ namaḥ
12	ॐ ऐं द्रौं नमः	oṃ aiṃ drauṃ namaḥ
13	ॐ ऐं श्रीं नमः	oṃ aiṃ śrīṃ namaḥ
14	ॐ ऐं त्रूं नमः	oṃ aiṃ trūṃ namaḥ
15	ॐ ऐं व्रूं नमः	oṃ aiṃ vrūṃ namaḥ
16	ॐ ऐं फ्रें नमः	oṃ aiṃ phreṃ namaḥ
17	ॐ ऐं ह्रां नमः	oṃ aiṃ hrāṃ namaḥ
18	ॐ ऐं जुं नमः	oṃ aiṃ juṃ namaḥ
19	ॐ ऐं स्त्रौं नमः	oṃ aiṃ strauṃ namaḥ
20	ॐ ऐं स्लूं नमः	oṃ aiṃ slūṃ namaḥ

21	ॐ ऐं प्रें नमः	oṃ aiṃ preṃ namaḥ
22	ॐ ऐं ह्स्वां नमः	oṃ aiṃ hsvāṃ namaḥ
23	ॐ ऐं प्रीं नमः	oṃ aiṃ prīṃ namaḥ
24	ॐ ऐं फ्रां नमः	oṃ aiṃ phrāṃ namaḥ
25	ॐ ऐं क्रीं नमः	oṃ aiṃ krīṃ namaḥ
26	ॐ ऐं श्रीं नमः	oṃ aiṃ śrīṃ namaḥ
27	ॐ ऐं क्रां नमः	oṃ aiṃ krāṃ namaḥ
28	ॐ ऐं सः नमः	oṃ aiṃ saḥ namaḥ
29	ॐ ऐं क्लीं नमः	oṃ aiṃ klīṃ namaḥ
30	ॐ ऐं व्रें नमः	oṃ aiṃ vreṃ namaḥ
31	ॐ ऐं ईं नमः	oṃ aiṃ īṃ namaḥ
32	ॐ ऐं ज्स्ह्ल्रीं नमः	oṃ aiṃ jshlrīṃ namaḥ

ॐ ऐं ह्रीं नमः क्लीं ह्रीं फट् स्वाहा
oṃ aiṃ hrīṃ namaḥ klīṃ hrīṃ phaṭ svāhā

इति दशमोऽध्यायः
iti daśamo-dhyāyaḥ
Here ends Chapter Ten

अथ एकादशोऽध्यायः — atha ekādaśo-dhyāyaḥ

1	ॐ ऐं श्रौं नमः	oṃ aiṃ śrauṃ namaḥ
2	ॐ ऐं क्रूं नमः	oṃ aiṃ krūṃ namaḥ
3	ॐ ऐं श्रीं नमः	oṃ aiṃ śrīṃ namaḥ
4	ॐ ऐं ल्लीं नमः	oṃ aiṃ llīṃ namaḥ
5	ॐ ऐं प्रें नमः	oṃ aiṃ preṃ namaḥ
6	ॐ ऐं सौं नमः	oṃ aiṃ sauṃ namaḥ
7	ॐ ऐं स्हौं नमः	oṃ aiṃ shauṃ namaḥ
8	ॐ ऐं श्रूं नमः	oṃ aiṃ śrūṃ namaḥ
9	ॐ ऐं क्लीं नमः	oṃ aiṃ klīṃ namaḥ
10	ॐ ऐं स्क्लीं नमः	oṃ aiṃ sklīṃ namaḥ
11	ॐ ऐं प्रीं नमः	oṃ aiṃ prīṃ namaḥ
12	ॐ ऐं ग्लौं नमः	oṃ aiṃ glauṃ namaḥ
13	ॐ ऐं ह्स्ह्रीं नमः	oṃ aiṃ hshrīṃ namaḥ
14	ॐ ऐं स्तौं नमः	oṃ aiṃ stauṃ namaḥ
15	ॐ ऐं लीं नमः	oṃ aiṃ līṃ namaḥ
16	ॐ ऐं म्लीं नमः	oṃ aiṃ mlīṃ namaḥ
17	ॐ ऐं स्तूं नमः	oṃ aiṃ stūṃ namaḥ
18	ॐ ऐं ज्स्ह्रीं नमः	oṃ aiṃ jshnīṃ namaḥ
19	ॐ ऐं फ्रूं नमः	oṃ aiṃ phrūṃ namaḥ
20	ॐ ऐं क्रूं नमः	oṃ aiṃ krūṃ namaḥ

21	ॐ ऐं ह्रीं नमः	oṃ aiṃ hrīṃ namaḥ
22	ॐ ऐं ल्लूं नमः	oṃ aiṃ llūṃ namaḥ
23	ॐ ऐं क्ष्म्रीं नमः	oṃ aiṃ kṣmrīṃ namaḥ
24	ॐ ऐं श्रूं नमः	oṃ aiṃ śrūṃ namaḥ
25	ॐ ऐं इं नमः	oṃ aiṃ iṃ namaḥ
26	ॐ ऐं जुं नमः	oṃ aiṃ juṃ namaḥ
27	ॐ ऐं त्रैं नमः	oṃ aiṃ traiṃ namaḥ
28	ॐ ऐं द्रूं नमः	oṃ aiṃ drūṃ namaḥ
29	ॐ ऐं ह्रौं नमः	oṃ aiṃ hrauṃ namaḥ
30	ॐ ऐं क्लीं नमः	oṃ aiṃ klīṃ namaḥ
31	ॐ ऐं सूं नमः	oṃ aiṃ sūṃ namaḥ
32	ॐ ऐं हौं नमः	oṃ aiṃ hauṃ namaḥ
33	ॐ ऐं श्व्रं नमः	oṃ aiṃ śvraṃ namaḥ
34	ॐ ऐं व्रूं नमः	oṃ aiṃ vrūṃ namaḥ
35	ॐ ऐं फां नमः	oṃ aiṃ phāṃ namaḥ
36	ॐ ऐं ह्रीं नमः	oṃ aiṃ hrīṃ namaḥ
37	ॐ ऐं लं नमः	oṃ aiṃ laṃ namaḥ
38	ॐ ऐं ह्सौं नमः	oṃ aiṃ hsauṃ namaḥ
39	ॐ ऐं सें नमः	oṃ aiṃ seṃ namaḥ
40	ॐ ऐं ह्रीं नमः	oṃ aiṃ hrīṃ namaḥ
41	ॐ ऐं ह्रौं नमः	oṃ aiṃ hrauṃ namaḥ

42	ॐ ऐं विं नमः	oṃ aiṃ viṃ namaḥ
43	ॐ ऐं प्लीं नमः	oṃ aiṃ plīṃ namaḥ
44	ॐ ऐं क्ष्म्क्लीं नमः	oṃ aiṃ kṣmklīṃ namaḥ
45	ॐ ऐं त्स्रां नमः	oṃ aiṃ tsrāṃ namaḥ
46	ॐ ऐं प्रं नमः	oṃ aiṃ praṃ namaḥ
47	ॐ ऐं म्लीं नमः	oṃ aiṃ mlīṃ namaḥ
48	ॐ ऐं स्रूं नमः	oṃ aiṃ srūṃ namaḥ
49	ॐ ऐं क्ष्मां नमः	oṃ aiṃ kṣmāṃ namaḥ
50	ॐ ऐं स्तूं नमः	oṃ aiṃ stūṃ namaḥ
51	ॐ ऐं स्ह्रीं नमः	oṃ aiṃ shrīṃ namaḥ
52	ॐ ऐं थ्प्रीं नमः	oṃ aiṃ thprīṃ namaḥ
53	ॐ ऐं क्रौं नमः	oṃ aiṃ krauṃ namaḥ
54	ॐ ऐं श्रां नमः	oṃ aiṃ śrāṃ namaḥ
55	ॐ ऐं म्लीं नमः	oṃ aiṃ mlīṃ namaḥ

ॐ ऐं ह्रीं क्लीं श्रीं सौं नमः फट् स्वाहा

oṃ aiṃ hrīṃ klīṃ śrīṃ sauṃ namaḥ phaṭ svāhā

इत्येकादशोऽध्यायः

ityekādaśo-dhyāyaḥ

Here ends Chapter Eleven

अथ द्वादशोऽध्यायः — atha dvādaśo-dhyāyaḥ

1	ॐ ऐं ह्रीं नमः	oṃ aiṃ hrīṃ namaḥ
2	ॐ ऐं ओं नमः	oṃ aiṃ oṃ namaḥ
3	ॐ ऐं श्रीं नमः	oṃ aiṃ śrīṃ namaḥ
4	ॐ ऐं ईं नमः	oṃ aiṃ īṃ namaḥ
5	ॐ ऐं क्लीं नमः	oṃ aiṃ klīṃ namaḥ
6	ॐ ऐं क्रूं नमः	oṃ aiṃ krūṃ namaḥ
7	ॐ ऐं श्रूं नमः	oṃ aiṃ śrūṃ namaḥ
8	ॐ ऐं प्रां नमः	oṃ aiṃ prāṃ namaḥ
9	ॐ ऐं क्रूं नमः	oṃ aiṃ krūṃ namaḥ
10	ॐ ऐं दिं नमः	oṃ aiṃ diṃ namaḥ
11	ॐ ऐं फ्रें नमः	oṃ aiṃ phreṃ namaḥ
12	ॐ ऐं हं नमः	oṃ aiṃ haṃ namaḥ
13	ॐ ऐं सः नमः	oṃ aiṃ saḥ namaḥ
14	ॐ ऐं चें नमः	oṃ aiṃ ceṃ namaḥ
15	ॐ ऐं सूं नमः	oṃ aiṃ sūṃ namaḥ
16	ॐ ऐं प्रीं नमः	oṃ aiṃ prīṃ namaḥ
17	ॐ ऐं व्लूं नमः	oṃ aiṃ vlūṃ namaḥ
18	ॐ ऐं आं नमः	oṃ aiṃ āṃ namaḥ
19	ॐ ऐं औं नमः	oṃ aiṃ auṃ namaḥ
20	ॐ ऐं ह्रीं नमः	oṃ aiṃ hrīṃ namaḥ

21	ॐ ऐं क्रीं नमः	oṃ aiṃ krīṃ namaḥ
22	ॐ ऐं द्रां नमः	oṃ aiṃ drāṃ namaḥ
23	ॐ ऐं श्रीं नमः	oṃ aiṃ śrīṃ namaḥ
24	ॐ ऐं स्लीं नमः	oṃ aiṃ slīṃ namaḥ
25	ॐ ऐं क्लीं नमः	oṃ aiṃ klīṃ namaḥ
26	ॐ ऐं स्लूं नमः	oṃ aiṃ slūṃ namaḥ
27	ॐ ऐं ह्रीं नमः	oṃ aiṃ hrīṃ namaḥ
28	ॐ ऐं व्लीं नमः	oṃ aiṃ vlīṃ namaḥ
29	ॐ ऐं त्रों नमः	oṃ aiṃ troṃ namaḥ
30	ॐ ऐं ओं नमः	oṃ aiṃ oṃ namaḥ
31	ॐ ऐं श्रौं नमः	oṃ aiṃ śrauṃ namaḥ
32	ॐ ऐं ऐं नमः	oṃ aiṃ aiṃ namaḥ
33	ॐ ऐं प्रें नमः	oṃ aiṃ preṃ namaḥ
34	ॐ ऐं द्रूं नमः	oṃ aiṃ drūṃ namaḥ
35	ॐ ऐं क्लूं नमः	oṃ aiṃ klūṃ namaḥ
36	ॐ ऐं औं नमः	oṃ aiṃ auṃ namaḥ
37	ॐ ऐं सूं नमः	oṃ aiṃ sūṃ namaḥ
38	ॐ ऐं चें नमः	oṃ aiṃ ceṃ namaḥ
39	ॐ ऐं ह्रूं नमः	oṃ aiṃ hrūṃ namaḥ

40	ॐ ऐं प्लीं नमः	oṃ aiṃ plīṃ namaḥ
41	ॐ ऐं क्षां नमः	oṃ aiṃ kṣāṃ namaḥ

ॐ यं यं यं रं रं रं ठं ठं ठं फट् स्वाहा

oṃ yaṃ yaṃ yaṃ raṃ raṃ raṃ ṭhaṃ ṭhaṃ ṭhaṃ phaṭ svāhā

इति द्वादशोऽध्यायः

iti dvādaśo-dhyāyaḥ

Here ends Chapter Twelve

अथ त्रयोदशोऽध्यायः atha trayodaśo-dhyāyaḥ

1	ॐ ऐं श्रौं नमः	oṃ aiṃ śrauṃ namaḥ
2	ॐ ऐं व्रीं नमः	oṃ aiṃ vrīṃ namaḥ
3	ॐ ऐं ओं नमः	oṃ aiṃ oṃ namaḥ
4	ॐ ऐं औं नमः	oṃ aiṃ auṃ namaḥ
5	ॐ ऐं ह्रां नमः	oṃ aiṃ hrāṃ namaḥ
6	ॐ ऐं श्रीं नमः	oṃ aiṃ śrīṃ namaḥ
7	ॐ ऐं श्रां नमः	oṃ aiṃ śrāṃ namaḥ
8	ॐ ऐं ओं नमः	oṃ aiṃ oṃ namaḥ
9	ॐ ऐं प्लीं नमः	oṃ aiṃ plīṃ namaḥ
10	ॐ ऐं सौं नमः	oṃ aiṃ sauṃ namaḥ
11	ॐ ऐं ह्रीं नमः	oṃ aiṃ hrīṃ namaḥ
12	ॐ ऐं क्रीं नमः	oṃ aiṃ krīṃ namaḥ
13	ॐ ऐं ल्लूं नमः	oṃ aiṃ llūṃ namaḥ
14	ॐ ऐं क्लीं नमः	oṃ aiṃ klīṃ namaḥ
15	ॐ ऐं ह्रीं नमः	oṃ aiṃ hrīṃ namaḥ
16	ॐ ऐं प्लीं नमः	oṃ aiṃ plīṃ namaḥ
17	ॐ ऐं श्रीं नमः	oṃ aiṃ śrīṃ namaḥ
18	ॐ ऐं ल्लीं नमः	oṃ aiṃ llīṃ namaḥ
19	ॐ ऐं श्रूं नमः	oṃ aiṃ śrūṃ namaḥ
20	ॐ ऐं ह्रीं नमः	oṃ aiṃ hrīṃ namaḥ

21	ॐ ऐं त्रूं नमः	oṃ aiṃ trūṃ namaḥ
22	ॐ ऐं ह्रीं नमः	oṃ aiṃ hrīṃ namaḥ
23	ॐ ऐं ह्रां नमः	oṃ aiṃ hrāṃ namaḥ
24	ॐ ऐं प्रीं नमः	oṃ aiṃ prīṃ namaḥ
25	ॐ ऐं ॐ नमः	oṃ aiṃ oṃ namaḥ
26	ॐ ऐं सूं नमः	oṃ aiṃ sūṃ namaḥ
27	ॐ ऐं ह्लौं नमः	oṃ aiṃ hlauṃ namaḥ
28	ॐ ऐं षौं नमः	oṃ aiṃ ṣauṃ namaḥ
29	ॐ ऐं आं ल्क्रीं नमः	oṃ aiṃ āṃ lkrīṃ namaḥ
30	ॐ ऐं ओं नमः	oṃ aiṃ oṃ namaḥ

ऐं ह्रीं क्लीं चामुण्डायै विच्चे
aiṃ hrīṃ klīṃ camuṇḍayai vicce

इति त्रयोदशोऽध्यायः
iti trayodaśo-dhyāyaḥ
Here ends Chapter Thirteen

इति तन्त्ररूपेणपरिणता श्रीतन्त्रदुर्गासप्तशती समाप्त
iti tantrarūpeṇapariṇatā śrītantradurgāsaptaśatī samāpta
Thus ends the full and complete Tantrik form
of Śrī Tantra Durgā Saptaśatī

तन्त्ररूपन्देवी सूक्तम् tantrarūpandevī sūktam

1	ॐ ऐं ह्सों नमः	oṃ aiṃ hsoṃ namaḥ
2	ॐ ऐं ह्रीं नमः	oṃ aiṃ hrīṃ namaḥ
3	ॐ ऐं श्रीं नमः	oṃ aiṃ śrīṃ namaḥ
4	ॐ ऐं हूं नमः	oṃ aiṃ hūṃ namaḥ
5	ॐ ऐं क्लीं नमः	oṃ aiṃ klīṃ namaḥ
6	ॐ ऐं रौं नमः	oṃ aiṃ rauṃ namaḥ
7	ॐ ऐं स्त्रीं नमः	oṃ aiṃ strīṃ namaḥ
8	ॐ ऐं म्लीं नमः	oṃ aiṃ mlīṃ namaḥ
9	ॐ ऐं प्लूं नमः	oṃ aiṃ plūṃ namaḥ
10	ॐ ऐं स्हौं नमः	oṃ aiṃ shauṃ namaḥ
11	ॐ ऐं स्त्रीं नमः	oṃ aiṃ strīṃ namaḥ
12	ॐ ऐं ग्लूं नमः	oṃ aiṃ glūṃ namaḥ
13	ॐ ऐं व्रीं नमः	oṃ aiṃ vrīṃ namaḥ
14	ॐ ऐं सौं नमः	oṃ aiṃ sauṃ namaḥ
15	ॐ ऐं लूं नमः	oṃ aiṃ lūṃ namaḥ
16	ॐ ऐं ल्लूं नमः	oṃ aiṃ llūṃ namaḥ
17	ॐ ऐं द्रां नमः	oṃ aiṃ drāṃ namaḥ
18	ॐ ऐं क्सां नमः	oṃ aiṃ ksāṃ namaḥ
19	ॐ ऐं क्ष्म्रीं नमः	oṃ aiṃ kṣmrīṃ namaḥ
20	ॐ ऐं ग्लौं नमः	oṃ aiṃ glauṃ namaḥ

21	ॐ ऐं स्कं नमः	oṃ aiṃ skaṃ namaḥ
22	ॐ ऐं त्रूं नमः	oṃ aiṃ trūṃ namaḥ
23	ॐ ऐं स्क्लूं नमः	oṃ aiṃ sklūṃ namaḥ
24	ॐ ऐं क्रौं नमः	oṃ aiṃ krauṃ namaḥ
25	ॐ ऐं श्रीं नमः	oṃ aiṃ śrīṃ namaḥ
26	ॐ ऐं म्लूं नमः	oṃ aiṃ mlūṃ namaḥ
27	ॐ ऐं क्लूं नमः	oṃ aiṃ klūṃ namaḥ
28	ॐ ऐं शां नमः	oṃ aiṃ śāṃ namaḥ
29	ॐ ऐं ल्हीं नमः	oṃ aiṃ lhīṃ namaḥ
30	ॐ ऐं स्रूं नमः	oṃ aiṃ srūṃ namaḥ
31	ॐ ऐं ल्लीं नमः	oṃ aiṃ llīṃ namaḥ
32	ॐ ऐं लीं नमः	oṃ aiṃ līṃ namaḥ
33	ॐ ऐं सं नमः	oṃ aiṃ saṃ namaḥ
34	ॐ ऐं लूं नमः	oṃ aiṃ lūṃ namaḥ
35	ॐ ऐं ह्सूं नमः	oṃ aiṃ hsūṃ namaḥ
36	ॐ ऐं श्रूं नमः	oṃ aiṃ śrūṃ namaḥ
37	ॐ ऐं जूं नमः	oṃ aiṃ jūṃ namaḥ
38	ॐ ऐं ह्स्ल्रीं नमः	oṃ aiṃ hslrīṃ namaḥ
39	ॐ ऐं स्क्रीं नमः	oṃ aiṃ skrīṃ namaḥ
40	ॐ ऐं क्लां नमः	oṃ aiṃ klāṃ namaḥ
41	ॐ ऐं श्रूं नम	oṃ aiṃ śrūṃ nama

42	ॐ ऐं हं नमः	oṃ aiṃ haṃ namaḥ
43	ॐ ऐं ह्लीं नमः	oṃ aiṃ hlīṃ namaḥ
44	ॐ ऐं क्स्रूं नमः	oṃ aiṃ ksrūṃ namaḥ
45	ॐ ऐं द्रौं नमः	oṃ aiṃ drauṃ namaḥ
46	ॐ ऐं क्लूं नमः	oṃ aiṃ klūṃ namaḥ
47	ॐ ऐं गां नमः	oṃ aiṃ gāṃ namaḥ
48	ॐ ऐं सं नमः	oṃ aiṃ saṃ namaḥ
49	ॐ ऐं ल्स्रां नमः	oṃ aiṃ lsrāṃ namaḥ
50	ॐ ऐं फ्रीं नमः	oṃ aiṃ phrīṃ namaḥ
51	ॐ ऐं स्लां नमः	oṃ aiṃ slāṃ namaḥ
52	ॐ ऐं ल्लूं नमः	oṃ aiṃ llūṃ namaḥ
53	ॐ ऐं फ्रें नमः	oṃ aiṃ phreṃ namaḥ
54	ॐ ऐं ओं नमः	oṃ aiṃ oṃ namaḥ
55	ॐ ऐं स्म्लीं नमः	oṃ aiṃ smlīṃ namaḥ
56	ॐ ऐं ह्रां नमः	oṃ aiṃ hrāṃ namaḥ
57	ॐ ऐं ॐ नमः	oṃ aiṃ oṃ namaḥ
58	ॐ ऐं ह्लूं नमः	oṃ aiṃ hlūṃ namaḥ
59	ॐ ऐं हूं नमः	oṃ aiṃ hūṃ namaḥ
60	ॐ ऐं नं नमः	oṃ aiṃ naṃ namaḥ
61	ॐ ऐं स्रां नमः	oṃ aiṃ srāṃ namaḥ
62	ॐ ऐं वं नमः	oṃ aiṃ vaṃ namaḥ

63	ॐ ऐं मं नमः	oṃ aiṃ maṃ namaḥ
64	ॐ ऐं म्क्लीं नमः	oṃ aiṃ mklīṃ namaḥ
65	ॐ ऐं शां नमः	oṃ aiṃ śāṃ namaḥ
66	ॐ ऐं लं नमः	oṃ aiṃ laṃ namaḥ
67	ॐ ऐं भौं नमः	oṃ aiṃ bhauṃ namaḥ
68	ॐ ऐं ल्लूं नमः	oṃ aiṃ llūṃ namaḥ
69	ॐ ऐं हौं नमः	oṃ aiṃ hauṃ namaḥ
70	ॐ ऐं ईं नमः	oṃ aiṃ īṃ namaḥ
71	ॐ ऐं चें नमः	oṃ aiṃ ceṃ namaḥ
72	ॐ ऐं ल्क्रीं नमः	oṃ aiṃ lkrīṃ namaḥ
73	ॐ ऐं ह्ल्रीं नमः	oṃ aiṃ hlrīṃ namaḥ
74	ॐ ऐं क्ष्म्ल्रीं नमः	oṃ aiṃ kṣmlrīṃ namaḥ
75	ॐ ऐं पूं नमः	oṃ aiṃ pūṃ namaḥ
76	ॐ ऐं श्रौं नमः	oṃ aiṃ śrauṃ namaḥ
77	ॐ ऐं ह्रौं नमः	oṃ aiṃ hrauṃ namaḥ
78	ॐ ऐं भ्रूं नमः	oṃ aiṃ bhrūṃ namaḥ
79	ॐ ऐं क्स्त्रीं नमः	oṃ aiṃ kstrīṃ namaḥ
80	ॐ ऐं आं नमः	oṃ aiṃ āṃ namaḥ
81	ॐ ऐं क्रूं नमः	oṃ aiṃ krūṃ namaḥ
82	ॐ ऐं त्रूं नमः	oṃ aiṃ trūṃ namaḥ

इति तन्त्ररूपन्देवीसूक्तम्

iti tantrarūpandevīsūktam

Here ends the Tantrik Form of the Praise of the Goddess

हरिविरञ्चिमहेश्वरपूजिताम्
भगवतीञ्जनदुर्गतिहारिणीम् ।
सकलतन्त्रमयीञ्जगदीश्वरीं
सुखमयीञ्जगताञ्जननीं भजे ॥ १ ॥

harivirañcimaheśvarapūjitām
bhagavatīñjanadurgatihāriṇīm I
sakalatantramayīñjagadīśvarīṃ
sukhamayīñjagatāñjananīṃ bhaje II 1 II

She who is worshipped by Viṣṇu, Brahma and Siva; the Supreme Goddess who destroys difficulties for living beings; who is the Embodiment of all Synthesis; the Ruler of Manifestation; the Embodiment of Joy, the Mother of all Existences, it is She who I praise.

सर्वार्थंसाधनकरीम्महतीमुदारां
स्वर्गापवर्गगतिदांकरुणावताराम् ।
संसारतारणपरां हृतपापभारान्
दुर्गान्नमामि शिरसाऽहमनन्तसाराम् ॥ २ ॥

sarvārthaṃsādhanakarīmmahatīmudārāṃ
svargāpavargagatidāṃkaruṇāvatārām I
saṃsāratāraṇaparāṃhṛtapāpabhārān durgānnamāmi
śirasā-hamanantasārām II 2 II

The Objective of all spiritual discipline; Greatness; Distinction; Giver of progress towards the realm of divinity and Self Realization; the Incarnations of Compassion; the Safe Passage beyond the Sea of Objects and Relationships; who takes away the burden of mistakes and misgivings; I bow my head to the Remover of Difficulties, to the Eternal Essence.

इति श्रीतन्त्रदुर्गासप्तशती

iti śrītantradurgāsaptaśatī

Here ends the Respected Synthesis of The Seven Hundred Verses of She Who Removes All Difficulties.

paramadevī sūktam

oṃ asya śrīparamadevatāsūktamālāmantrasya mārkaṇḍeya sumedhādi-ṛṣayaḥ, gāyatryādinānāvidhāni chandāṃsi, triśaktirūpiṇī caṇḍikā devatā, aiṃ bījaṃ sauḥ śaktiḥ klīṃ kīlakaṃ caturvidhapuruṣārthasiddhyarthe jape viniyogaḥ I

oṃ yogāḍhyāmarakāyanirgatamahattejaḥ samutpattinī
bhāsvatpūrṇaśaśāṃkacāruvadanā nīlollasadbhrūlatā II
gaurottuṃgakucadvayā tadupari sphūrjaprabhāmaṇḍalā
bandhūkāruṇakāyakāntiravatācchrīcaṇḍikā sarvataḥ II

oṃ aiṃ hrīṃ śrīṃ hskhphreṃ hsauṃ hsauḥ jaya jaya mahālakṣmi jagadādhārabīje surāsuratribhuvananidhāne dayāṅkure sarvatejorūpiṇi mahāmahāmahime mahāmahārūpiṇi mahāmahāmāye mahāmāyāsvarūpiṇi viriñcasaṃstute vidhivarade cidānande (vidyānande) viṣṇudehāvṛte mahāmohamohini madhukaiṭabhajighāṃsini nityavaradānatatpare mahāsudhābdhivāsini mahāmahattejodhāriṇi sarvādhāre sarvakāraṇakāraṇe acintyarūpe indrādinikhilanirjarasevite sāmagānagāyini pūrṇodayakāriṇi vijaye jayanti aparājite sarvasundari raktāṃśuke sūryakoṭisaṃkāśe candrakoṭisuśītale agnikoṭidahanaśīle yamakoṭikrūre vāyukoṭivahanasuśīle oṃkāranādacidrupe nigamāgamamārgadāyini mahiṣāsuranirdalani dhūmralocanavadhaparāyaṇe caṇḍamuṇḍādiśiraśchedini nikhilāsurabalakhādini tridaśarājyadāyini sarvastrīratnarūpiṇi divyadehe nirguṇe sadasadrūpadhāriṇi skandavarade (suravarade) bhaktatrāṇatatpare varavarade sahastrāre daśaśatākṣare ayutākṣare saptakoṭicāmuṇḍārūpiṇi navakoṭikātyāyanirūpiṇi anekaśaktyā lakṣyālakṣyasvarūpe indrāṇi brahmāṇi rudrāṇi kaumāri vaiṣṇāvi vārāhi śivadūti īśāni bhīme bhrāmari nārasiṃhi trayastriṃśatkoṭidaivate anantakoṭibrahmāṇḍanāyike caturaśītilakṣamunijanasaṃstute saptakoṭimantrasvarūpe mahākālarātriprakāśe kalākāṣṭhādirūpiṇi caturdaśabhuvanāvirbhavakāriṇi garuḍagāmini krauṅkāra-hrauṅkāra-hrīṅkāra-śrīṅkāra-kṣoṅkāra-jūṅkāra-sauṅkāra-aiṅkāra-klīṅkāra-hlīṅkāra- hlāṅkāra - hauṅkāra-nānābījamantra rājavirājita sakalasundarīgaṇasevita caraṇāravinde śrīmahārātri-tripurasundari-kāmeśadayite karuṇārasakallolini kalpavṛkṣādhaḥsthite cintāmaṇidvīpādasthita-maṇimandiranivāse cāpini khaḍgini cakriṇi gadini śaṅkhini padmini nikhilabhairavārādhite samastayoginīcakraparivṛte kāli kaṅkāli tāre totule sutāre jvālāmukhi chinnamastake bhuvaneśvari tripure trilokajanani viṣṇuvakṣaḥsthalālaṅkāriṇi ajite amite aparājite anaupamacarite garbhavāsādiduḥkhāpahāriṇi muktikṣetrādhiṣṭhāyini śive śānti kumāri devi devīsūktasaṃstute mahākāli mahālakṣmi mahāsarasvati trayīvigrahe prasīda prasīda sarvamanorathān pūraya pūraya sarvariṣṭavighnāṃśchedaya chedaya sarvagrahapīḍājvarograbhayaḥ vidhvaṃsaya vidhvaṃsaya sadyastribhuvanajīvajātaṃ vaśamānaya vaśamānaya mokṣamārgaṃ darśaya darśaya jñānamārgaṃ prakāśaya prakāśaya ajñānatamo nirasaya nirasaya dhanadhānyābhivṛddhiṃ kuru kuru sarvakalyāṇāni kalpaya kalpaya māṃ rakṣa rakṣa mama vajraśarīraṃ sādhaya sādhaya aiṃ hrīṃ klīṃ cāmuṇḍāyai vicce svāhā namaste namaste namaste svāhā I

paraṃ devyā idaṃ sūktaṃ yaḥ paṭhetprayato naraḥ I
sarvasiddhimavāpnoti sarvatra vijayī bhavet II 1 II

saṃgrāmeṣu japecchatrūn mataṅgāniva kesarī I
vaśayennikhilānlokān viśeṣeṇa mahīpatīn II 2 II

trikālaṃ ca paṭhennityaṃ devyāḥ sūktamidaṃ param I
tasyavighnāḥ pralīyante grahapīḍaśca dāruṇāḥ II 3 II

jvarādirogaśamanaṃ parakṛtyānivāraṇam I
parābhicāraśamanaṃ tīvradāridrya nāśanam II 4 II

parakalyāṇanilayaṃ devyāḥ santoṣakārakam I
sahasrāvṛttito devi manorathasiddhidam II 5 II

dvisahasrāvṛttijapātsarvasaṃkaṣṭanāśanam I
trisahasrāvṛttitastu vaśakṛdrājayoṣitām II 6 II

śatatrayaṃ paṭhedyastu varṣatrayamatandritaḥ I
sa paśyeccaṇḍikāṃ sākṣād varadānakṛtodyamām II 7 II

idaṃ rahasyaṃ paramaṃ gopanīyaṃ prayatnataḥ I
na vācyaṃ kasyaciddevi nidhānamiva sundari II 8 II

śrījagadambārpaṇamastu II iti paramadevī-sūktam II

aparājitā stotram

oṃ śuddhasphaṭika-saṃkāśāṃ candrakoṭi suśītalām I
abhaya-varadahastāṃ śuklavastrairalaṃkṛtām II

nānābharaṇasaṃyuktāṃ cakravākaiśca veṣṭhitām I
evaṃ dhyāyet samāsīno ya etāmaparājitām II

oṃ asya aparājitā-mantrasya nārada vedavyāsa ṛṣiranuṣṭupchandaḥ śrīaparājitā devatā lakṣmī bījaṃ bhuvaneśvarī śaktirmama sarvābhīṣṭasiddhyarthe jape viniyogaḥ I

mārkaṇḍeya uvāca

śṛṇudhvaṃ munayaḥ sarve sarvakāmārthasiddhidām I
asiddhasādhinīṃ devīṃ vaiṣṇavīmaparājitām II

oṃ namo bhagavate vāsudevāya namo'stvanantāya sahasraśīrṣāya kṣīrodārṇavaśāyine I

śeṣabhogaparyaṃkāya garuḍavāhanāya ajāya ajitāya amitāya aparājitāya pītavāsase vāsudeva śaṃkarṣaṇa pradyumna aniruddha hayagrīva mahāvarāha narasiṃha vāmana trivikrama rāma rāma śrīrāma matsya kurma varaprada namo-stu te svāhā I

oṃ namo-stu te sura-daitya-dānava-nāga-gandharva-yakṣa-rākṣasa-bhūta-preta- piśāca-kuṣmāṇḍa-siddha-yoginī-ḍākinī-skanda-purogān graha nakṣatradoṣān doṣāṃścānyān hana hana daha daha paca paca matha matha vidhvaṃsaya vidhvaṃsaya vicūrṇaya vicūrṇaya vidrāvaya vidrāvaya śaṅkhena cakreṇa vajreṇa khaṅgena śūlena gadayā mūṣalena halena dāmodara bhasmīkuru kuru svāhā ।

oṃ sahasrabāho sahasrapraharaṇāyudha jaya jaya vijaya vijaya ajita ajita amita amita aparājitā apratihata sahasranetra jvala jvala prajvala prajvala virūpa viśvarūpa bahurūpa madhusūdana mahāvarāha acyuta nṛsiṃha mahāpuruṣa puruṣottama vaikuṇṭha nārāyaṇa padmanābha govinda aniruddha dāmodara hṛṣīkeśa keśava vāmana sarvasurotsādana sarvabhūtabhayaṃkara sarvaśatrupramardana sarvamantra-prabhañjana sarvaroga-praṇāśana sarvanāga-pramardana sarvadeva-maheśvara sarvabandhavimokṣaṇa sarvāhita-pramardana sarvahiṃsrapradamana sarvajarapraṇāśana sarvagraha-nivāraṇa sarvapāpapramardana ḍākinīvidhvaṃsana sarvaduḥsvapnanāśana janārdana namo-stu te svāhā ।

ya īmāmaparājitāṃ paramavaiṣṇavīṃ paṭhati vidyāṃ smarati siddhāṃ mahāvidyāṃ japati paṭhati śṛṇoti smārayati dhārayati kīrttayati vācayati vā gṛhītvā haste pathi gacchati vā bhaktyā likhitvā gṛhe sthāpayati vā tasya nāgni-vāyu-vajro-palā'śanibhayaṃ na varṣabhayaṃ na śatrubhayaṃ na corabhayaṃ na sarpabhayaṃ na svāpadabhayaṃ na samudrabhayaṃ na rājabhayaṃ vā bhavet ॥

na tasya rātryandhakāra-strī-rājakūla-viṣopaviṣa garalahana- vaśīkaraṇavidveṣaṇoccāṭana-vadha-bandhanabhayaṃ vā bhavet I
ebhirmantrairudāhṛtaiḥ siddhaiḥ saṃsiddhapūjitaiḥ II

tadyathā I

oṃ namaste-stu abhaye anaghe ajite amite apare aparājite paṭhati siddhe vidye smarati siddhe mahāvidye aikānaṃśe ume dhruve arundhati sāvitri gāyatri jātavedasi mānastoke sarasvati dhamaṇi dhāmaṇi ramaṇi rāmaṇi dharaṇi dhāraṇi saudāmini aditi diti vinate gauri gāndhāri śabari kirātini mātaṃgi kṛṣṇe yaṣode satyavādini brahmavādini kāli kapālini karālini karālanetre bhīmanādinī vikarālanetre sadyopacayakari mātaḥ sarvayācanavarade śubhade arthade sādhini apamṛtyuṃ nāśaya nāśaya pāpaṃ hara hara jalagataṃ sthalagataṃ antarīkṣagataṃ māṃ rakṣa rakṣa sarvabhūtasarvopadravebhyaḥ svāhā II

yasyāḥ praṇaśyate puṣpaṃ garbho vā patate yadi I
mriyante bālakāḥ yasyāḥ kākavandhyā ca yā bhavet II

bhūrjapatre tvimāṃ vidyāṃ likhitvā dhārayet sadā I
aibhirdoṣairna lipyeta śubhagā putriṇī bhavet II

bhūrjapatre kuṃkumena likhitvā dhārayettu yaḥ I
raṇe rājakūle dyūte saṃgrāme ripusaṃkule II

agnicaurabhaye ghore nityaṃ tasya jayo bhavet I
śastrañca vārayatyeṣā samaye kāṇḍadhāriṇī II

gulma-śūlākṣirogāṇāṃ kṣipraṃ nāśayate vyathām I
śirorogajvarāṇāñca nāśinīṃ sarvadehinām II

tadyathā - aikāhika-dvyāhika-tryāhika-cāturthika-māsika-
dvaimāsika-traimāsika-cāturmāsika-ṣāṇmāsika-
mauhūrttika-vātika-paittika-ślaiṣmika-sānnipātika-jvara
satatajvara-santata-jvara viṣamajvara-
grahanakṣatradoṣāṃścānyān hara hara kāli śara śara
gauri dhama dhama vidye āle māle tāle bandhe paca paca
vidye matha matha vidye nāśaya nāśaya pāpaṃ hara hara
duḥsvapnaṃ vidhvaṃsaya vidhvaṃsaya vighnavināśini
rajani sandhye dundubhināde mānastoke mānasavege
śaṅkhiṇi cakriṇi vajriṇi gadini śūlini apamṛtyu-vināśini
viśveśvari draviḍhi drāviḍhi keśavadayite paśupatisahite
duḥkhadurante dundubhinādini bhīmamardini damani
dāmini śabari kirāti mātaṃgi māheśvari indrāṇi brahmāṇi
vārāhi māhendri kaumāri caṇḍi cāmuṇḍe namo'stu te I

oṃ hrāṁ hrīṁ hrūṁ hraiṁ hrauṃ hraḥ turu turu svāhā I

ye māṃ dviṣanti pratyakṣaṃ parokṣaṃ vā tān sarvān
hana hana daha daha paca paca mardaya mardaya tāpaya
tāpaya śoṣaya śoṣaya utsādaya utsādaya brahmāṇi
vaiṣṇavi māheśvari vārāhi kaumāri
vaināyaki aindri āgneyi caṇḍi cāmuṇḍe vāruṇi vāyavi
sarvakāmaphalaprade rakṣa rakṣa pracaṇḍavidye
indropendra-bhagini jaye vijaye śānti puṣṭhi-tuṣṭhi-

kīrttivivarddhini kāmāṃkuśe kāmadughe sarvakāmavarapradeh sarvabhūteṣu māṃ priyaṃ kuru kuru svāhā ।

oṃ hrīṁ hrīṁ hraṁ hraḥ ।

oṃ ākarṣiṇi āveśini jvālāmālini ramaṇi rāmaṇi dhamani dhāmani tapani tāpani mādanonmādini saṃśoṣiṇi mahākāli nīlapatāke mahārātri mahāgauri mahāmāye mahāśraye mahācāndri mahāśauri mahāmayuri ādityaraśmi jāhnavi yamaghaṇṭe ।

oṃ āṃ kilikili cintāmaṇi surabhi-surotpanne sarvakāmadughe yathābhilāṣitaṃ kāryaṃ tanme sidhyatu svāhā ।

oṃ ādite svāhā oṃ aparājite svāhā oṃ bhūḥ svāhā oṃ bhuvaḥ svāhā oṃ svaḥ svāhā oṃ bhūrbhuvaḥ svaḥ svāhā ।

ṣata evāgataṃ pāpaṃ tatraiva pratigacchatu svāhā ।
oṃ bale bale mahābale asiddhasādhini svāhā ॥

॥ oṃ iti viṣṇudharmottare tṛtīyakāṇḍe trailokya-vijayā-nāmāparājitā-stotraṃ samāptam oṃ ॥

śrīkuñjikāstotram

rī gaṇeśāya namaḥ

ṃ asya śrīkuñjikāstotramantrasya sadāśiva ṛṣiḥ anuṣṭup
handaḥ śrītriguṇātmikā devatā oṃ aiṃ bījaṃ oṃ hrīṃ
aktiḥ oṃ klīṃ kīlakaṃ mama sarvābhīṣṭasiddhyarthe
ape viniyogaḥ I

iva uvāca

ṇu deva pravakṣyāmi kuñjikāstotramuttamam I
ena mantraprabhāveṇa caṇḍījāpaḥ śubho bhavet II 1 II

a kavacaṃ nārgalāstotraṃ kīlakaṃ na rahasyakam I
a sūktaṃ nāpi vā dhyānaṃ na nyāso na vārcanam II 2 II

uñjikāpāṭhamātreṇa durgāpāṭhaphalaṃ labhet I
iguhyataraṃ devi devānāmapi durlabham II 3 II

opanīyaṃ prayatnena svayoniriva pārvati I
āraṇaṃ mohanaṃ vaśyaṃ stambhanoccāṭanādikam II 4 II

ṭhamātreṇa saṃsiddhyet kuñjikāstotramuttamam I
ṃ śrūṃ śrūṃ śrūṃ śaṃ phaṭ aiṃ hrīṃ klīṃ jvala ujjvala
ajvala hrīṃ hrīṃ klīṃ stravaya srāvaya śāpaṃ nāśaya
śaya śrīṃ śrīṃ śrīṃ jūṃ saḥ srāvaya ādaya svāhā II 5 II

oṃ śrlīṃ hūṃ klīṃ glāṃ jūṃ saḥ jvala ujjvala mantraṃ
prajvala haṃ saṃ laṃ kṣaṃ phaṭ svāhā I
namaste rudrarūpāyai namaste madhumardini II 6 II

namaste kaiṭabhanāśinyai namaste mahiṣārdini I
namaste śumbhahantryai ca niśumbhāsurasūdini II 7 II

namaste jāgrate devi jape siddhiṃ kurūṣva me I
aiṅkārī sṛṣṭirūpiṇyai hrīṅkārī pratipālikā II 8 II

klīṃ kālī kālarūpiṇyai bījarūpe namo-stu te I
cāmuṇḍā caṇḍarūpā ca yaiṅkārī varadāyinī II 9 II

vicce tvabhayadā nityaṃ namaste mantrarūpiṇi I
dhāṃ dhīṃ dhūṃ dhūrjaṭeḥ patnī vāṃ vīṃ vāgīśvarī tathā
II 10 II

krāṃ krīṃ krūṃ kuñjikā devi śrāṃ śrīṃ śrūṃ me
śubhaṃ kuru I
hūṃ hūṃ hūṅkārarūpiṇyai jrāṃ jrīṃ jrūṃ bhālanādinī II 11

bhrāṃ bhrīṃ bhrūṃ bhairavī bhadre bhavānyai te namo
namaḥ I
oṃ aṃ kaṃ caṃ ṭaṃ taṃ paṃ sāṃ vidurāṃ vidurāṃ
vimardaya vimardaya hrīṃ kṣāṃ kṣīṃ srīṃ jīvaya jīvaya
troṭaya troṭaya jambhaya jambhaya dīpaya dīpaya mocaya
mocaya hūṃ phaṭ jrāṃ vauṣaṭ aiṃ hrīṃ klīṃ rañjaya rañjay
sañjaya sañjaya guñjaya guñjaya bandhaya bandhaya bhrāṃ
bhrīṃ bhrūṃ bhairavī bhadre saṅkuca saṅkuca troṭaya
troṭaya mlīṃ svāhā II 12 II

ṃ pīṃ pūṃ pārvatī pūrṇā khāṃ khīṃ khūṃ khecarī tathā ।
nlāṃ mlīṃ mlūṃ mūlavastīrṇā kuñjikāstotrahetave ॥ 13 ॥

bhaktāya na dātavyaṃ gopitaṃ rakṣa pārvati ।
ihīnā kuñjikādevyā yastu saptaśatīṃ paṭhet ॥ 14 ॥

a tasya jāyate siddhirhyaraṇye ruditaṃ yathā ॥ 15 ॥

। iti śrīḍāmaratantre īśvarapārvatīsaṃvāde kuñjikāstotraṃ
ampūrṇam ॥

devipuṣpāñjalīstotram

ayi girinandini nanditamedini viśvavinodini nandinute
girivaravindhyaśiro'dhinivāsini viṣṇuvilāsini jiṣṇunute ।
bhagavati he śitikaṇṭhakuṭumbini bhūrikuṭumbini bhūtikṛte
jaya jaya he mahiṣāsuramardini ramyakapardini śailasute ॥ 1 ॥

suravaravarṣiṇi durdharadharṣiṇi durmukhamarṣiṇi harṣarate
tribhuvanapoṣiṇi śaṅkaratoṣiṇi kalmaṣamoṣiṇi ghoṣarate ।
danujaniroṣiṇi durmadaśoṣiṇi durmuniroṣiṇi sindhusute
jaya jaya he mahiṣāsuramardini ramyakapardini śailasute ॥ 2 ॥

ayi jagadamba kadambavana priyavāsini toṣiṇi hāsarate
śikhariśiromaṇituṅga himālayaśṛṅganijālayamadhyagate ।
madhumadhure madhukaiṭabhagañjini mahiṣavidāriṇi rāsarate
jaya jaya he mahiṣāsuramardini ramyakapardini śailasute ॥ 3 ॥

ayi nijahuṁkṛtimātranirākṛtadhūmravilocanadhūmraśate
samaraviśoṣitaroṣitaśoṇitabījasamudbhavabījalate ।
śivaśivaśumbhaniśumbhamahāhavatarpitabhūtapiśācarate
jaya jaya he mahiṣāsuramardini ramyakapardini śailasute ॥ 4 ॥

ayi śatakhaṇḍavikhaṇḍitaruṇḍavituṇḍitaśuṇḍagajādhipate
nijabhujadaṇḍanipātitacaṇḍavipāṭitamuṇḍabhaṭādhipate ।
ripugajagaṇḍavidāraṇacaṇḍaparākramaśauṇḍamṛgādhipate
jaya jaya he mahiṣāsuramardini ramyakapardini śailasute ॥ 5 ॥

dhanuranuṣaṅga ranakṣaṇasaṅga parisphuradaṅganaṭatkaṭake
kanakapiśaṅgapuṣpatkaniṣaṅgarasadbhaṭaśṛṅgahatābaṭuke
hatacaturaṅgabalakṣitiraṅgaghaṭadbahuraṅgaraṭadbaṭuke
jaya jaya he mahiṣāsuramardini ramyakapardini śailasute ॥6॥

ayi raṇadurmadaśatruvadhāddhuradurdharanirbharaśaktibhṛte
caturavicāradhurīṇamahāśayadūtakṛtapramathādhipate ।
duritadurīhadurāśayadurmatidānavadūtadurantagate
jaya jaya he mahiṣāsuramardini ramyakapardini śailasute ॥7॥

ayi śaraṇāgatavairivadhūjanavīravarābhayadāyikare
tribhuvanamastakaśūlavirodhiśirodhikṛtāmalaśūlakare ।
dumidumitāmaradundubhinādamuhurmukharīkṛtadiṅnikare
jaya jaya he mahiṣāsuramardini ramyakapardini śailasute ॥8॥

suralalanātatatheyitatheyitathābhinayottaranṛtyarate
kṛtakukuthākukuthodiḍadāḍikatālakutūhalagānarate
dhudhukuṭadhūdhuṭadhindhimitadhvanidhiramṛdaṅganinādarate
jaya jaya he mahiṣāsuramardini ramyakapardini śailasute ॥9॥

jaya jaya jāpyajaye jayaśabdaparastutitatparaviśvanute
jhaṇajhaṇajhiṃjhimajhiṃkṛtanūpuraśiñjitamohitabhūtapate ।
naṭitanaṭārdhanaṭīnaṭanāyakanāṭananāṭitanaṭyarate
jaya jaya he mahiṣāsuramardini ramyakapardini śailasute ॥10॥

ayi sumanaḥsumanaḥsumanaḥsumanaḥsumanoramakāntiyute
śritarajanīrajanīrajanīrajanīrajanīkaravaktrabhṛte ।
sunayanavibhramarabhramarabhramarabhramarabhramarābhidṛte
jaya jaya he mahiṣāsuramardini ramyakapardini śailasute ॥11॥

mahitamahāhavamallamatallikavallitarallitabhallirate
viracitaballikapālikapallikajhillikabhillikavargavṛte ।
śrutakṛtapullasamullasitāruṇatallajapallavasallalite
jaya jaya he mahiṣāsuramardini ramyakapardini śailasute ॥ 12 ॥

ayi sudatījanalālasamānasamohanamanmatharājasute
aviralagaṇḍagalanmadameduramattamattaṅgajarājagate ।
tribhuvanabhūṣaṇabhūtakalānidhirūpapayonidhirājasute
jaya jaya he mahiṣāsuramardini ramyakapardini śailasute ॥ 13 ॥

kamaladalāmalakomalakāntikalākalitāmalabhālatale
sakalavilāsakalānilayakramakelicalatkalahaṃsakule ।
alikulasaṅkulakuntalamaṇḍalamaulimiladbakulālikule
jaya jaya he mahiṣāsuramardini ramyakapardini śailasute ॥ 14 ॥

karamuralīravavīrjitakūjitalajjitakokilamañjumate
militamilindamanoharaguñjitarañjitaśailanikuñjagate ।
nijagaṇabhūtamahāśabarīgaṇaraṅgaṇasambhṛtakelirate
jaya jaya he mahiṣāsuramardini ramyakapardini śailasute ॥ 15 ॥

kaṭitaṭapītadukūlavicitramayūkhatiraskṛtacaṇḍaruce
jitakanakācalamaulimadorjita garjitakuñjarakumbhakuce ।
praṇatasurā'suramaulimaṇisphuradaṃśulasannakhacandraruce
jaya jaya he mahiṣāsuramardini ramyakapardini śailasute ॥ 16 ॥

vijitasahasrakaraikasahasrakaraikasahasrakaraikanute
kṛtasuratārakasaṅgaratārakasaṅgaratārakasūnunute ।
surathasamādhisamānasamādhisamāna samādhisujāpyarate
jaya jaya he mahiṣāsuramardini ramyakapardini śailasute ॥ 17 ॥

padakamalaṃ karuṇānilaye varivasyati yo-nudinaṃ suśive
ayi kamale kamalānilaye kamalānilayaḥ sa kathaṃ na bhavet I
tava padameva paraṃ padamastviti śīlayato mama kiṃ na śive
jaya jaya he mahiṣāsuramardini ramyakapardini śailasute II 18 II

kanakalasatkalaśīkajalairanuṣiñcati te-ṅgaṇaraṃgabhuvam
bhajati sa kiṃ na śacīkucakumbhanaṭīparirambhasukhānubhavam I
tava caraṇaṃ śaraṇaṃ karavāṇi suvāṇi pathaṃ mama dehi śivam
jaya jaya he mahiṣāsuramardini ramyakapardini śailasute II 19 II

tava vimalendukulaṃ vadanendumalaṃ kalayannanukūlayate
kimu puruhūtapurīndumukhīsumukhībhirasau vimukhīkriyate I
mama tu mataṃ śivamānadhane bhavatī kṛpayā kimu na kriyate
jaya jaya he mahiṣāsuramardini ramyakapardini śailasute II 20 II

ayi mayi dīnadayālutayā kṛpayaiva tvayā bhavitavyamume
ayi jagato jananīti yathā-si mayā-si tathā-numatāsi rame I
yaducitamatra bhavatpuragaṃ kuru śāmbhavi devi dayāṃ kuru me
jaya jaya he mahiṣāsuramardini ramyakapardini śailasute II 21 II

stutimimāṃ stimitaḥ susasamādhinā
niyamato yamato-nudinaṃ paṭhet I
paramayā ramayā sa niṣevyate
parijano-rijano-pi ca taṃ bhajet II 22 II

II iti devipuṣpāñjalīstotraṃ samāptam II

चण्डी माँ की आरती
caṇḍī mām̐ kī āratī
Be Victorious!

जय चण्डी जय जय (माँ) जय चण्डी जय जय
भयहारिणि भवतारिणि भवभामिनि जय जय
ॐ जय चण्डी जय जय

jaya caṇḍī jaya jaya (mām̐) jaya caṇḍī jaya jaya
bhayahāriṇi bhavatāriṇi bhavabhāmini jaya jaya
oṃ jaya caṇḍī jaya jaya

Be Victorious! Oh Goddess Who Tears Apart Thought! Be Victorious! You take away all fear and illuminate the intensity of reality. Be Victorious!

तू ही सत-चित-सुखमय शुद्ध ब्रह्मरूपा (माँ)
सत्य सनातन सुन्दर पर-शिव सूर-भूपा
ॐ जय चण्डी जय जय ॥ १ ॥

tū hī sata-cita-sukhamaya śuddha brahmarūpā (mām̐)
satya sanātana sundara para-śiva sūra-bhūpā
oṃ jaya caṇḍī jaya jaya ॥ 1 ॥

You are the essence of Truth, Consciousness, Happiness, the form of Pure Conscious Being. You are the beauty of Eternal Truth. Beyond infinite goodness, you rule over all the Gods. Be Victorious!

आदि अनादि अनामय अविचल अविनाशी (माँ)
अमल अनन्त अगोचर अज आनन्दराशी
ॐ जय चण्डी जय जय ॥ २ ॥

ādi anādi anāmaya avicala avināśī (mām̐)
amala ananta agocara aja ānandarāśī
oṃ jaya caṇḍī jaya jaya ॥ 2 ॥

The beginning, without beginning, unseverable; motionless and indestructible; Bright, infinite, imperceptible, unborn, the great collection of Bliss. Be Victorious!

अविकारी अघहारी अकल कलाधारी (माँ)
कर्त्ता विधि भर्त्ता हरि हर संहरकारी
ॐ जय चण्डी जय जय ॥३॥

avikārī aghahārī akala kalādhārī (māṁ)
karttā vidhi bharttā hari hara saṃharakārī
oṃ jaya caṇḍī jaya jaya ॥3॥

Changless, holy One, sinless, bearer of individual phenomena; created by Brahmā, sustained by Viṣṇu, and Śiva who dissolves this creation. Be Victorious!

तू विधि वधू रमा तू उमा महामाया (माँ)
मूलप्रकृति विद्या तू तू जननी जाया
ॐ जय चण्डी जय जय ॥४॥

tū vidhi vadhū ramā tū umā mahāmāyā (māṁ)
mūlaprakṛti vidyā tū tū jananī jāyā
oṃ jaya caṇḍī jaya jaya ॥4॥

You are the wife of Brahmā, the wife of Viṣṇu (Ramā), the wife of Śiva (Umā), the Great Measurement of Consciousness. You are the knowledge of primordial existence, the Mother who gives birth to all. Be Victorious!

राम कृष्ण तू सीता ब्रजरानी राधा (माँ)
तू वाञ्छाकल्पद्रुम हारिणि सब बाधा
ॐ जय चण्डी जय जय ॥५॥

rāma kṛṣṇa tū sītā brajarānī rādhā (māṁ)
tū vāñchākalpadruma hāriṇi saba bādhā
oṃ jaya caṇḍī jaya jaya ॥5॥

You are the consciousness of the subtle light of wisdom that merges with the Ultimate. You are the Doer of All. You are Sītā, the pure white one, the Queen of the multitude; Rādhā, the Ruler of all success. You are the desire of the wish-fulfiilling tree, taking away all obstructions. Be Victorious!

दश विद्या नव दुर्गा नानाशस्त्रकरा (माँ)

अष्टमातृका योगिनि नव नव रूप धरा

ॐ जय चण्डी जय जय ॥६॥

daśa vidyā nava durgā nānāśastrakarā (mām̐)
aṣṭamātṛkā yogini nava nava rūpa dharā
oṃ jaya caṇḍī jaya jaya ॥6॥

You are the ten braches of knowledge (Mahā Vidyās) and the nine Relievers of Difficulties (nine Durgās). All of the scriptures present you. The eight Mothers of union. Various are the forms that you assume. Be Victorious!

तू परधामनिवासिनि महाविलासिनि तू (माँ)

तु ही श्मशानविहारिणि ताण्डवलासिनि तू

ॐ जय चण्डी जय जय ॥७॥

tū paradhāmanivāsini mahāvilāsini tū (mām̐)
tu hī śmaśānavihāriṇi tāṇḍavalāsini tū
oṃ jaya caṇḍī jaya jaya ॥7॥

You are the inhabitant of the highest residence. Yours is the greatest beauty. You wander about the cremation grounds dancing to the rhythmic music. Be Victorious!

सुर मुनि मोहिनि सौम्या तू शोभाऽऽधारा (माँ)

विवसनविकट-सरूपा प्रलयमयी धारा

ॐ जय चण्डी जय जय ॥८॥

sura muni mohini saumyā tū śobhā--dhārā (mām̐)
vivasanavikaṭa-sarūpā pralayamayī dhārā
oṃ jaya caṇḍī jaya jaya ॥8॥

You mesmerize the Gods and munis when you present your radiant beauty. All are helpless seeing your dreadful appearance at the time when you assume the form of total dissolution. Be Victorious!

तू ही स्नेह-सुधामयि तू अति गरलमना (माँ)
रत्नविभूषित तू ही तू ही अस्थि तना
ॐ जय चण्डी जय जय ॥९॥

tū hī sneha-sudhāmayi tū ati garalamanā (mām̐)
ratnavibhūṣita tū hī tū hī asthi tanā
oṃ jaya caṇḍī jaya jaya ॥9॥

You pervade Love and ease. You are extremely eminent. You are the Brilliance of the jewel. You are the invisible existence. Be Victorious!

मूलाधारनिवासिनि इह पर सिद्धि प्रदे (माँ)
कालातीता काली कमल तू वरदे
ॐ जय चण्डी जय जय ॥१०॥

mūlādhāranivāsini iha para siddhi prade (mām̐)
kālātītā kālī kamala tū varade
oṃ jaya caṇḍī jaya jaya ॥10॥

You reside in the Mūlādhāra Chakra. You grant the highest attainment in this world. At the appointed time you are Kālī, the Remover of Darkness, and as the Lotus One you grant blessings. Be Victorious!

शक्ति शक्ति धर तू ही नित्य अभेदमयी (माँ)
भेदप्रदर्शिनि वाणी विमले वेदत्रयी
ॐ जय चण्डी जय जय ॥११॥

śakti śakti dhara tū hī nitya abhedamayī (mām̐)
bhedapradarśini vāṇī vimale vedatrayī
oṃ jaya caṇḍī jaya jaya ॥ 11 ॥

You are every form of energy, the eternal undistinguishable essence, the vibration that exposes change and distinction, and the spotlessly pure three Vedas. Be Victorious!

हम अति दीन दुखी (माँ) विपत्-जाल घेरे (माँ)

हैं कपूत् अति कपटी पर बालक तेरे

ॐ जय चण्डी जय जय ॥ १२ ॥

ham ati dīna dukhī (mām̐) vipat-jāla ghere (mām̐)
haiṃ kapūt ati kapaṭī para bālaka tere
oṃ jaya caṇḍī jaya jaya ॥ 12 ॥

For so many days we have been in pain, Maa. We are bound by adversities and suffering. We arer negligent and insincere, but still we are your children. Be Victorious!

निज स्वभाववश जननी दया दृष्टि कीजै (माँ)

करुणा कर करुणामयि चरण-शरण दीजै

ॐ जय चण्डी जय जय ॥ १३ ॥

nija svabhāvavaśa jananī dayā dṛṣṭi kījai (mām̐)
karuṇā kara karuṇāmayi caraṇa-śaraṇa dījai
oṃ jaya caṇḍī jaya jaya ॥ 13 ॥

Endow us with your very own nature, Mother. Give us your mercy, Oh Merciful Mother! Give us the refuge of your lotus feet. Be Victorious!

जय चण्डी जय जय (माँ) जय चण्डी जय जय

भयहारिणि भवतारिणि भवभामिनि जय जय

ॐ जय चण्डी जय जय

jaya caṇḍī jaya jaya (māṁ) jaya caṇḍī jaya jaya
bhayahāriṇi bhavatāriṇi bhavabhāmini jaya jaya
oṃ jaya caṇḍī jaya jaya

Be Victorious! Oh Goddess Who Tears Apat Thought! Be Victorious! You take away all fear and illuminate the intensity of reality. Be Victorious!

देवीमयी

devīmayī

Manifestation of the Goddess

तव च का किल न स्तुतिरम्बिके
सकलशब्दमयीकिल ते तनुः ।
निखिलमूर्तिषु मे भवदन्वयो
मनसिजासु बहिःप्रसरासु च ॥

tava ca kā kila na stutirambike
sakalaśabdamayīkila te tanuḥ ।
nikhilamūrtiṣu me bhavadanvayo
manasijāsu bahiḥprasarāsu ca ॥

Oh Mother! Is there any vibration that is not your song? Your body is the form of all sound. In cognizing your imminent form of divinity, my mind has moved beyond thoughts and reflections.

इति विचिन्त्य शिवे शमिताशिवे
जगति जातमयत्नवशादिदम् ।
स्तुतिजपार्चनचिन्तनवर्जिता
न खलु काचन कालकलास्ति मे ॥

iti vicintya śive śamitāśive
jagati jātamayatnavaśādidam ।
stutijapārcanacintanavarjitā
na khalu kācana kālakalāsti me ॥

Oh Destroyer of all Obstructions, Grantor of Welfare! Recognizing you as such, as She who gives birth to all that moves and moves not, even these brief moments of my appearance in life should be spent without other thoughts in singing your praises, chanting your names, and offering of my devotion.

भगवतीस्तुतिः

bhagavatīstutiḥ

A Song of Praise to the Supreme Goddess

प्रातः स्मरामि शरदिन्दुकरोज्ज्वलाभां

सद्रत्नवन्मकरकुण्डलहारभूषाम् ।

दिव्यायुधोजितसुनीलसहस्रहस्तां

रक्तोत्पलाभचरणां भवतीं परेशाम् ॥

prātaḥ smarāmi śaradindukarojjvalābhāṃ

sadratnavanmakarakuṇḍalahārabhūṣām ।

divyāyudhojitasunīlasahasrahastāṃ

raktotpalābhacaraṇāṃ bhavatīṃ pareśām ॥

In the morrnng I remember the Foremost, She who shines like the autumn moon, wearing a shining necklace and earrings studded with fine jewels. She holds divine weapons in Her thousand arms of excellent blue, She gives divine life. The soles of her feet are red like a lotus. She is the Highest Divinity.

प्रातर्नमामि महिषासुरचण्डमुण्ड-

शुम्भासुरप्रमुखदैत्यविनाशदक्षाम् ।

ब्रह्मेन्द्ररुद्रमुनिमोहनशीललीलां

चण्डीं समस्तसुरमूर्तिमनेकरूपाम् ॥

prātarnamāmi mahiṣāsuracaṇḍamuṇḍa-

śumbhāsurapramukhadaityavināśadakṣām ।

brahmendrarudramunimohanaśīlalīlāṃ

caṇḍīṃ samastasuramūrtimanekarūpām ॥

In the morning I bow down to the Foremost, to the Slayer of the Great Ego, Anger and Passion, and the Destroyer of other negativities of duality led by Self-Conceit. Her graceful activities delude even Brahmā, the Creative Consciousness, Indra, the Rule of the Pure, Rudra, the Reliever of Sufferings, and other wise beings. She is Chaṇḍī, She Who Tears Apart Thought, the image of divinity to all the Gods in so many forms.

प्रातर्भजामि भजतामभिलाषदात्रीं

धात्रीं समस्तजगतां दुरितापहन्त्रीम् ।

संसारबन्धनवमोचनहेतुभूतां

मायां परां समधिगम्य परस्य विष्णोः ॥

prātarbhajāmi bhajatāmabhilāṣadātrīṃ

dhātrīṃ samastajagatāṃ duritāpahantrīm ।

saṃsārabandhanavamocanahetubhūtāṃ

māyāṃ parāṃ samadhigamya parasya viṣṇoḥ ॥

In the morning I laud the Foremost, the Fulfiller of All Desires for those who worship, the Creator of all the worlds and Remover of all difficulties. Take away all bondage from the world of objects and relationships, and bring us to the pure intuitive vision of the Supreme Consciousness that resides beyond Māyā.

प्रणामः

praṇāmaḥ

Bowing Down with Devotion

ॐ दुर्गां शिवां शन्तिकरीं ब्रह्माणीं ब्रह्मणः प्रियां ।

सर्वलोक प्रणेत्रीञ्च प्रणमामि सदा शिवाम् ॥

oṃ durgāṃ śivāṃ śantikarīṃ
brahmāṇīṃ brahmaṇaḥ priyāṃ I
sarvaloka praṇetrīñca praṇamāmi sadā śivām II

The Reliever of Difficulties, Exposer of Goodness, Cause of Peace, Infinite Consciousness, Beloved by Knowers of Consciousness, She who Motivates and Guides the three worlds, always I bow to Her, and I am bowing to Goodness Herself.

मङ्गलां शोभनां शुद्धां निष्कलां परमां कलाम् ।

विश्वेश्वरीं विश्वमातां चण्डिकां प्रणमाम्यहम् ॥

maṅgalāṃ śobhanāṃ śuddhāṃ
niṣkalāṃ paramāṃ kalām I
viśveśvarīṃ viśvamātāṃ
caṇḍikāṃ praṇamāmyaham II

Welfare, Radiant Beauty, Completely Pure, without limitatioins, the Ultimate Limitation, the Lord of the Universe, the Mother of the Universe, to you Chaṇḍī, to the Energy that Tears Apart Thought, I bow in submission.

सर्वदेवमयीं देवीं सर्वरोगभयापहाम् ।

ब्रह्मेशविष्णुनमितां प्रणमामि सदाशिवां ॥

sarvadevamayīṃ devīṃ sarvarogabhayāpahām I
brahmeśaviṣṇunamitāṃ praṇamāmi sadāśivāṃ II

She is composed of all the Gods, removes all sickness and fear, Brahmā, Maheśvara, and Viṣṇu bow down to Her, and I always bow down to the Energy of Infinite Goodness.

विन्ध्यस्तां विन्ध्यनिलयां दिव्यस्थाननिवासिनीम् ।

योगिनीं योगजननीं चण्डिकां प्रणमाम्यहम् ॥

vindhyasthāṃ vindhyanilayāṃ divyasthānanivāsinīm I
yoginīṃ yogajananīṃ caṇḍikāṃ praṇamāmyaham II

The dwelling place of Knowledge, residing in Knowledge, Resident in the place of Divine Illumination, the Cause of Union, the Knower of Union, to the Energy That Tears Apat Thought, we constantly bow.

ईशानमातरं देवीमीश्वरीमीश्वरप्रियाम् ।

प्रणतोऽस्मि सदादुर्गां संसारार्णवतारिणीम् ॥

īśānamātaraṃ devīmīśvarīmīśvarapriyām I
praṇato-smi sadādurgāṃ saṃsārārṇavatāriṇīm II

The Mother of the Supreme Consciousness, the Goddess Who is the Supreme Consciousness, beloved by the Supreme Consciousness, we always bow to Durgā, the Reliever of Difficulties, who takes aspirants across the difficult sea of objects and their relationships.

ॐ महादेव महात्राण महायोगि महेश्वर ।

सर्वपापहरां देव मकाराय नमो नमः ॥

oṃ mahādeva mahātrāṇa mahāyogi maheśvara I
sarvapāpaharāṃ deva makārāya namo namaḥ II

oṃ The Great God, the Great Reliever, the Great Yogi, Oh Supreme Lord, Oh God who removes all Sin, in the form of the letter "M" which dissolves creation, we bow to you again and again.

ॐ नमः शिवाय शान्ताय कारणत्रय हेतवे ।

निवेदयामि चात्मानं त्वं गतिः परमेश्वर ॥

oṃ namaḥ śivāya śāntāya kāraṇatraya hetave |
nivedayāmi cātmānaṃ tvaṃ gatiḥ parameśvara ||

oṃ I bow to the Consciousness of Infinite Goodness, to Peace, to the Cause of the three worlds, I offer to you the fullness of my soul, Oh Supreme Lord.

॥ इति बीजमन्त्रात्मक तन्त्रदुर्गासप्तशती सम्पूर्णम् ॥

|| iti bījamantrātmaka tantradurgā saptaśatī sampūrṇam ||

Thus is the completion of the Tantra Durgā Saptaśatī Bījamantrātmaka

Paramadevī Sūktam
The Song of the Supreme Goddess

Oṃ Presenting the garland of mantras composed as the Song of the Respected Supreme Goddess; Mārkaṇḍeya, Sumedha, and others are the Ṛṣis; Gāyatri and others of various rhythms are the chandas; the Intrinsic Nature of the Three Energies of Chaṇḍī is the Deity; Aiṃ (Wisdom) is the seed; Sauḥ (the Manifestation of all Existence, Prakṛti) is the Energy; Klīṃ (the cause of manifested existence merging into the causal body in perfection) is the pin; for the perfection of the four known objectives of human existence (dharma, artha, kāma, mokṣa) is the application for which these mantras are being applied in recitation.

She rides upon the embodiment of the Great Light of the union that is continually expanding. Her face is completely illuminated by the rising light of the Blue Moon. She who is Rays of Light is shining brightly, and above her and surrounding her is a halo of radiant light. The family member who is always the embodiment of the most beautiful manifestation of That is the Respected Chaṇḍī.

Oṃ - The Infinite Beyond Conception
Aiṃ - Wisdom
Hrīṃ - All of Maya
Śrīṃ - The perfection of Peace in the Mind and in the Heart
Hskphreṃ - The gross body, knowledge, sword of wisdom, fruits, vibrations, subtle body, wisdom, perfection;
Hsauṃ - The gross body, knowledge, divine perfection;
Hsauḥ - The gross body, knowledge, divine nature;
Be victorious, be victorious
The Great Goal of All Existence
Who is the primary seed of all manifested existence
Who is the substratum of all positives and negatives in the three worlds
Who is compassionate even to the cruel
Who is the Intrinsic Nature of all Light
Who is the Great Manifestation of all the Great
Who is the Intrinsic Nature of the Greatest of all the Great
Who is the Great Measurement of Consciousness of the Greatest of all the Great
Who is the Intrinsic Nature of the Great Measurement of Consciousness of the Greatest of all the Great
Who is sung of as being Various
Who is the Giver of the Boons of Discipline
Who is the Bliss of Consciousness

Who is the Bliss of Intelligence
Who is the movements in the body of He who pervades All
Who is the Cause of the delusion of the Great Ignorance caused by Attachment
Who puts Too Much and Too Little into Balance
Who eternally grants infinite boons
Who resides in the Great Purity
Who supports the Great Light of the Great
Who supports all
Who is the Cause of all Causes
Who wears the Unthinkable Form
Who is always engaged in the seva of Indra and other Divine Beings;
Who sings the songs of the Sāma Veda
Who is the cause of complete upliftment
Who is Unconquerable
Who is Victorious
Who is Undefeatable
Who is All Beauty
Who holds a sword covered with blood
Who disseminates the Light of ten million Suns
Who has the cooling rays of ten million Moons
Who has the burning power of ten million Fires
Who is as cruel as ten million Lords of Death
Who has the carrying capacity of ten million Lords of the Wind
Who is the form of the Consciousness of the subtle body of Oṃ
Who is the giver of the paths of the nigamas and āgamas propounded by Śakti and Śiva;
Who is the Slayer of the Great Ego
Who always destroys Sinful Eyes
Who cuts the heads from Anger and Passion
Who removes the capacity from the Seed of Desire and others
Who loves to drink Passion
Who is the Great One
Who is always in Union
Who is the Giver of Satisfaction to ghosts, goblins, and other terrifying ones
Who cuts the heads from Self Conceit and Self Deprecation
Who devours the strength from all thoughts of Duality
Who is the Giver of the Kingdom of the Three Worlds
Who is the Intrinsic Nature of the Jewels of all Women
Who has a Divine Body
Who is beyond all Qualities or Attributes
Who is the Support of the form of the Truth of all Truth

Who gives the blessing to Skanda (Commander of the Armies of the Gods)
Who gives the blessing to all the Gods
Who immediately takes devotees across (the ocean of Worldliness)
Who is the Giver of the Boon of all Boons
Who dwells in the crown chakra
Who has One Thousand Eyes
Who has Infinite Eyes
Who is the Intrinsic Nature of seventy million Goddesses who Destroy Anger and Passion
Who is the Intrinsic Nature of ninety million Goddesses who are Eternally Pure
Who embodies all Energies
Whose form is both Definable and Undefinable
Who is the Goddess who is the Ruler of the Pure
Who is the Goddess of Creative Capacity
Who is the Goddess who Destroys Negativity
Who is the Goddess who is Ever Pure
Who is the Goddess who Pervades All
Who is the Goddess who is the Boar of Sacrifice
Who is the Goddess for whom Consciousness is Emissary
Who is the Goddess who Rules over All
Who is the Goddess who is Terribly Frightful
Who is the Goddess who comes in the form of bees
Who is the Goddess who is half-human and half-lion
Who is the Goddess who is expressed through thirty-three million forms of divinity
Who presides as the Leader of Infinite Worlds
Who has been sung about by uncountable beings of wisdom since the dawn of creation
Who is the Intrinsic Nature of seventy million mantras
Who is the Illumination of the Great Night of Ignorance
Who is the Intrinsic Nature of all moments of Time
Who is the Cause of the Appearance of Forty Worlds
Who travels on Garuda, the King of Birds
Who is the subtle body of the Cause of Oṃ
Who is the manifestation of the Consciousness of the subtle body of the Cause of Oṃ
Who is Hrīṃ, all of Māyā in the gross body, subtle body, causal body and beyond
Who is Śrīṃ, the perfection of peace in our minds and hearts
Who is Kṣoṃ, the cause of the ultimate expression of Oṃ
Who is Jūṃ, Pure Consciousness
Who is Sauṃ, the Knowledge of perfect Divinity
Who is Aiṃ, Wisdom

Who is Klīṃ, the cause of perfection in manifested existence and the causal body
Who is Hlīṃ, the manifestation of perfection in the gross and causal bodies
Who is Hlāṃ, the the manifestation of perfect consciousness in the gross body
Who is Hauṃ, the gross body of Divinity
Who is expressed by various bīja mantras the Ruler of the Kingdom
Who is all beauty
Whose lotus feet are served by the multitudes of existence
Who is the Respected Great Night
Who is the Beautiful One of the Three Cities
Who fulfills all desires
Who is expressed in the sentiment of Compassion
Who resides in the tree which causes All Fulfillment
Who is situated on the Island of the Jewels of all thought
Who resides in the Temple of the mind
Who crushes opponents
Who wields a sword
Who holds a discus
Who displays a club
Who holds a conch shell
Who holds a lotus flower
Who can be extremely frightening
Who is encircled by all the Yoginis
Who is beyond Time
Who displays skulls
Who takes across
Whose tongue stutters
Who has excellent illumination
Whose face is luminous, or who is like a volcano
Who has severed Her own head
Who is the Supreme Lord of the earth
Who is in the three worlds
Who is the Mother of the three words
Who is an ornament on the breast of He Who Pervades the Universe
Who is Unconquerable
Who is Unmeasurable
Who is Undefeatable
Whose adventures are Infinite
Who takes away the pains of birth
Who establishes in the field of Liberation
Who is Goodness

Who is Peace
Who is the Goddess who is Ever Pure
Who is sung about in the hymns of the Goddess
Who is Mahākālī, Mahālakṣmī, and Mahāsaraswatī
Who is manifested in the three forms

Be pleased, be pleased
Make full, complete, and perfect the pure contemplations of the pure mind
Cut asunder all negative relationships, tear apart, tear apart
Destroy all pain, fear, and affliction caused by negative planetary influences, destroy, destroy
Make all living beings in the three worlds adhere to Truth,
Cause them to behave, cause them to behave
Show the path to Liberation, show, show
Illuminate the path of Wisdom, illuminate, illuminate
Remove all hope from the darkness of ignorance, remove, remove
Give everyone sufficient wealth and food, give, give
Make everyone contemplate the welfare of all,
contemplate, contemplate
Protect me, protect
Make my body as hard as diamonds, purify, purify
Aiṃ Hrīṃ Klīṃ Cāmuṇḍāyai Vicce, we bow to you, we bow to you, we bow to you I am One with God!

-1-

Whatever human will recite this hymn of the Supreme Goddess, will attain all perfection and become victorious in every encounter.

-2-

He or she will be victorious over all enemies in any confrontation, and will view all thoughts with the courage of a lion. He or she will always make their will prevail over all beings, especially over the Lords of the Earth.

-3-

Who will always recite this hymn of the Supreme Goddess at the three times of prayer, from him or her all obstacles will flee, even the pains caused by negative positions of the planets.

-4-

Disease and pains, etc. caused by old age will be removed from those who do (recitation to the Supreme), and the Supreme will think to destroy even painful afflictions.

-5-

The Goddess grants the supreme welfare, and is the Cause of all Satisfaction. For those who recite one thousand times, the Goddess brings all desires to perfection.

-6-

For those who recite two thousand times, all doubts will be destroyed. For those who recite three thousand times, they can control the actions of the king in His Kingdom.

-7-

Those who recite three hundred times and contemplate for three years time will see the actual Goddess Chaṇḍī granting the highest boons.

-8-

This is a Supreme Secret; make effort to protect it. The Goddess has revealed this to our Consciousness only as the gift of the One Most Beautiful.

-9-

Make this as an offering to the Respected Goddess who is the Mother of the Perceivable Existence.

Thus concludes the Song of the Supreme Goddess.

Aparājitā Stotram

The Song of She Who Cannot be Defeated

Appearing with the brilliance of pure crystal, emanating the cooling rays of ten million moons, with Her hands She is granting boons and freedom from fear, wearing a light colored cloth and ornaments.

With various accouterments, displaying the discus of revolving time and other weapons, we meditate upon She who cannot be defeated.

Oṃ, and now the mantras of She who cannot be defeated, Nārada and Veda Vyasa are the ṛṣis, anuṣṭup is the meter (32 syllables to the verse), the Respected She Who Cannot be Defeated is the Goddess, Lakṣmī is the seed, the Supreme Goddess of the Earth is the energy, for the perfection and fulfillment of all that is desirable is the application for which this recitation is being made.

Mārkaṇḍeya said:

Listen, Oh all you great Wise Ones, to that which grants the perfect fulfillment of the objects of all desires, the praise of the Goddess of Pure Discipline, the Energy of She Who Pervades the Universe, She who cannot be defeated.

Oṃ we bow to the Supreme Manifestation of Divinity, Lord of the Earth; We bow to the Infinite One, who has a Thousand Heads, who rests at the end of the infinite ocean of pure consciousness.

Who enjoys the bed of the Ultimate, whose conveyance is the eagle who is the King of Birds, who is Unborn, Undefeatable, without limitation, who cannot be defeated, dressed in yellow, Lord of the Earth, who is alert and apprehensive, who is the preeminent Mighty One, Unobstructed, who has a horse's head, the Great Boar of Sacrifice, the Man-lion of Courage, who came as a Dwarf, who performs all the Action of the Three Worlds, who is Rāma, Rāma - the perfect manifestation of the subtle body of consciousness, the Respected Rāma, who came as a fish, a tortoise, who Grants Boons, we bow to You, I am One with God.

Oṃ we bow to You who manifests the Great Strength of the Gods, those of duality, negative ties or bonds, snakes and other lowly beings, celestial musicians, Lords of Wealth, selfish beings with pride, ghosts, goblins, disembodied spirits, those with false conceptions, attained ones, Goddesses of Union, demonical energies, Kārttikeya - Commander of the armies of the Gods, Leader among the Planets, the faults of the Planets and Asterisms, various other faults, destroy, destroy, burn, burn, bring to perfection, bring to perfection, churn, churn, destroy, destroy, grind to powder, grind to powder, disperse, disperse, with your conch, your discus, your thunderbolt, your sword, your spear, your club, your pestle, your plow, Oh Giver of Compassion, turn it to ashes, do it, please do it, I am One with God!

Oṃ with a thousand arms, a thousand weapons of war, be victorious, be victorious, conquer, conquer, Oh Unconquerable One, Unconquerable One, Unlimited One, Unlimited One, who cannot be defeated, with no one before you, with a thousand shining eyes, shining, brilliantly, brilliantly, without form, the form of the universe, of many forms, who exudes sweetness, the great Boar of Sacrifice, Infinite One, the Man-lion of Courage, the great full and complete Consciousness, who dwells in the highest heaven, Manifestation of Consciousness, from whose navel comes a lotus, who is one-pointed light, Unobstructed, Giver of Compassion, Controller of the Senses, who Embodies Creation, Preservation, Transformation; Dwarf, the discipline of all the Gods, who instills fear in all ghosts and disembodied spirits, who defeats all enemies, who pronounces all mantras, who cures all disease, who destroys all snakes, who is the Great Supreme Lord of all Gods, who liberates from all bonds, who destroys all adversity, who controls all enmity, who destroys the incapacities of old age, who keeps the planets in proper orbit, who destroys all sin, who destroys Inimical Energies, who destroys bad dreams, who is above manifested existence, we bow to You, I am One with God!

This is the song of She Who Cannot be Defeated, the Supreme who Pervades the Universe; who reads, recites, remembers this knowledge becomes an attained one of great knowledge. Who continually recites, reads, hears, remembers, supports, inspires others to hear, explains, or even keeps this writing in his or her house, or in his or her hands while moving on the path, and with devotion establishes this writing in his or her house, to him or her there will be no fear from fire, wind, or lightning. He or she will be protected from Shani (malevolent planetary influences) and will not experience any fear, not from rain, enemies, thieves, snakes, the ocean, the king, nor from anyone or anything else!

No fear will come to him or her from the darkness of night, from attachment to the opposite sex, from the King or his family, and those individuals will be set free from death by poison, control by others, division, servitude, death, bondage, and others.

With these mantras he or she will become uplifted, delighted, become an attained one, and worthy of worship.

Thusly:

Oṃ We bow to you who grants freedom from fear, who is Undefeatable, Unlimited, with no one above, who cannot be defeated, who is the attainment of perfection in recitation, who is knowledge, who is remembered, who is the attainment of all perfection, who is the great knowledge, who is the One, who is the circumstance, who is consistent, who comes as Arundhatī, Sāvitri, Gāyatrī, the knower of all thoughts, as Saraswatī, who blows all like the wind, who causes all to blow, who enjoys with delight, who causes all to rejoice with delight, who holds aloft and supports all, who causes all to hold aloft and support all, who illuminates like lightning, who is beyond duality, who is duality, who is humble, who is Rays of Light, who Supports the Essence, who is simplicity, fame, the embodiment of thought, who is dark, who is welfare, who speaks truth, who speaks for the Supreme Divinity, who takes away Darkness, who wears a garland of skulls, who is formidable, who has formidable eyes, who makes a terrible sound, whose eyes instill fear, who offers truth, the Mother, who gives the blessings of all behavior, who grants purity, who grants meaning, who supports truth, beyond death, destroy, destroy, all sin take away, take away, that committed in waters, that committed on land, that committed in the atmosphere, protect me, protect all the elements from all opposition, I am One with God!

We children descended from the womb of existence, desiring the death of all bondage, bow to all of these with flowers.

This knowledge should be written on birch tree bark and always worn (in an amulet), by means of which all faults will be purified for yourselves and your children.

If this is written with red vermillion powder on birch bark and worn, it will bring delight and freedom from fear of the family of the king, in battle, in confrontation, and from the multitude of personal limitations (desire, anger, greed, illusion, ignorance, and jealousy).

There will be no fear from fire, thieves, or other violence, and he or she will be eternally victorious. It restrains opposing weapons and restricts divisions of time.

It will destroy the pain caused by opposing armies bearing dangerous weapons and destroy the pain of disease and old age in the entire body.

In this way: One recitation, two recitations, three recitations, four recitations, one month of recitations, two months of recitations, three months of recitations, four months of recitations, six months of recitations, even lasting for a moment, with a breath of the wind, coming from the bile, coming from the phlegm, not knowing the meaning, constantly reciting, reciting with joy, reciting irregularly, for the faults of the planets, asterisms, and others, take away, take away, Kālī, in constant motion, in constant motion, Gauri, blowing, blowing, Knowledge, in thorns, in objects of value, in clods of dirt, all bonds, with purifying, purifying knowledge, churning, churning, knowledge, destroy, destroy all sin, take away, take away, bad dreams, destroy, destroy, Oh Destroyer of all Obstacles, the night, the union with the sounds of the kettle drums, the manifestation of all thoughts, the agitation of all thoughts, you who hold the conch, the discus, the thunderbolt, the club, the spear, Destroyer of untimely Death, the Supreme Goddess of the Universe, pursuing, causing others to pursue, Manifestation of Creation, Preservation and Destruction, who is with the Lord of Animals, who removes all pain, who is the sound of the drum, Slayer of the Terrible, who has self-control, who causes others to have self-control, whose patience breeds humility, fame, the manifestation of mind, the Supreme Goddess of Consciousness, the Female Ruler of the Pure, the Energy of the Creative Consciousness, the Boar of Sacrifice, the Great Goddess of Consciousness, the Goddess of Purity, She Who Tears Apart Thoughts, the Slayer of Passion and Anger, we bow down to You!

Oṃ the Infinite beyond conception: the manifestation of the subtle body of consciousness: in the gross body, the causal body, the circumstance of all beings, in the body of all that is knowable, in the body of light, in the body of truth, consciousness, and bliss, strongly, powerfully proceed, I am One with God!

All of these enemies are constantly attacking me, and I request that you slay them, slay them, burn them, burn them, purify them, purify them, kill them, kill them, apply the heat of your purity, apply the heat of your purity, purify them, purify them, make them true, make them true, the Energy of the Creative Capacity, She who resides in All, the Great Supreme Seer of All, the Boar of Sacrifice, the Ever Pure One, the Great Remover of Obstacles, the Supreme Ruler of Purity, the Light of Purification, She Who Tears Apart Thoughts, the Slayer of Passion and Meanness, She who manifests in the Waters, She who manifests in the Wind, the Grantor of the fruits of All Desires, protect, protect, the knowledge which Tears Apart Thoughts, the Supreme Rule of the Pure, and She who almost (or approximates) the Supreme Rule of the Pure, the Goddess of Fortune, be victorious, conquer, bring Peace, Increase, Satisfaction, Fame, Progress, the Satisfaction of all Desires, grant the boon of all desires, which are beloved by Me, within all existence, do, do, I am One with God!

Oṃ the infinite beyond conception, Māyā, Māyā, Manifested Divinity, the Ultimate Divinity!

Oṃ She who attracts all, She who is Totally Independent, She who cultivates Illumination, She who is delightful, She who causes delight, who blows, who causes to blow, who is purifying austerities, who causes purifying austerities, who is intoxicating delight, who causes intoxicating delight, who is the balance of all, the Great Remover of Darkness, who has a blue flag, the great night, the great Goddess of Light, the Great Measurement of Consciousness, the Great Refuge, the Great Cause of Devotion, the Great Purity, the great peacock, She who Illuminates Non-duality, who is the restrained sound of the Ganges.

Oṃ Consciousness, the pin, the pin, the gem of all thought, of great strength, who gives birth to great strength, who yields all desires, and all desirable effects, bring to me the fruition, I am One with God!

Oṃ to She who is Non-duality, I am One with God!
Oṃ to She who Cannot be Defeated, I am One with God!
Oṃ to all that can be perceived through the senses, I am One with God!
Oṃ to all that can be conceived in the mind, I am One with God!
Oṃ to all that can be known through intuition or meditation, I am One with God! Oṃ the gross body, the subtle body, and the causal body, I am One with God!

The six (limitations) which give rise to sin we offer to you, I am One with God!

Oṃ One of strength, One of strength, One of great strength, the successful attainment of spiritual discipline, I am One with God!

Oṃ thus ends the Aparājitā Stotram, which can conquer the three worlds, which comes from the third part of the scripture known as The Highest Ideals of Viṣṇu.

Śrī Kuñjikā Stotram

The Respected Song which gives the Key to Perfection

We bow to the Respected Gaṇeśa, Lord of Wisdom, Lord of the Multitudes

Oṃ and now, presenting the mantras of the Respected Song which gives the Key to Perfection, the full, complete and eternal Consciousness of Infinite Goodness is the Ṛṣi, Anuṣṭup (32 syllables to the verse) is the meter, the capacity of the Respected Soul of the three qualities to manifest is the divinity, Oṃ Aiṃ (Wisdom) is the seed, Oṃ Hrīṃ (all of Māyā: what can be perceived in the gross body, the subtle body, the causal body and beyond) is the energy, Oṃ Klīṃ is the pin, for the perfection of all of my goals is the application of this recitation.

Śiva said:

-1-

Listen, oh Goddess, as I elucidate the excellent song which gives the key to perfection. By means of these mantras the recitation of Chaṇḍī becomes easy or illuminated.

-2-

Not the armor, nor the song which opens the bolt, nor the pin, nor the secrets; not the hymns, nor the meditations, nor establishment of the mantras within, nor the offerings;

-3-

merely by recitation of the Song That Gives the Key to Perfection will one gain the fruits of the sadhana (spiritual discipline) of Durgā. Oh Goddess, it is extremely secretive and difficult for even the gods to attain.

-4-

Even though it is secret, with right effort, oh you who were born from your own womb, Pārvati, Māraṇa (the capacity to slay anger, passion, and the Ego), Mohana (to become stupefied knowing none other than the Goddess), Vaśīkāraṇa (to make the mind sit still), Stambhana (to restrain the senses from wandering), Ucchātana (to become solely absorbed in the attainment of enlightenment), and all other attainments,

-5-

all come to perfection by means of the recitation of the excellent mantras of the Song That Gives the Key to Perfection.

Oṃ - the infinite beyond conception
śrūṃ - the perfection of peace in the circumstances of the mind
Śrūṃ - the perfection of peace in the circumstances of the mind
Śrūṃ - the perfection of peace in the circumstances of the mind
Śaṃ - Peace
Phaṭ - Purity
Aiṃ - Wisdom
Hrīṃ - Māyā, what can be perceived in the gross body, the subtle body, the causal body and beyond
Klīṃ - The cause of dissolving manifested existence in the perfection of the causal body
to burn brightly, more brightly,
Hrīṃ hrīṃ klīṃ
within all women, causing to flow, curses, destroy, destroy
Śrīṃ - the perfection of peace in the mind and heart
Śrīṃ - the perfection of peace in the mind and heart
Śrīṃ - the perfection of peace in the mind and heart
Jūṃ saḥ - Pure Consciousness
causing to flow together with other divinities
I am One with God!

Oṃ - the infinite beyond conception
Śrlīṃ - the perfection of peace in the gross body, subtle body, and causal body
Hūṃ - cut the ego
Klīṃ - The cause of dissolving manifested existence in the perfection of the causal body
Glāṃ - the perfection of wisdom in manifested existence
Jūṃ saḥ - Pure Consciousness
to burn brightly, these mantras
(and this) Illumination
Haṃ - (is the) Divine I
Saṃ - in all
Laṃ - manifested beings
Kṣaṃ - (to) the end of existence
Phaṭ - Purity
Svāhā - I am One with God!

We bow to the form of the Reliever from Sufferings, we bow to the Slayer of Too Much.

-7-

We bow to the Destroyer of Too Little, we bow to the Slayer of the Great Ego. We bow to the Slayer of Self-Conceit, and the destroyer of Self-Deprecation and others.

-8-

We bow to the Goddess who is awake and aware. Give me the attainment of perfection in recitation. In the form of Aiṃ, She is the potential form of creation, in the form of Hrīṃ, She protects all.

-9-

Klīṃ is the Goddess Kālī, the potential form of Time; in the form of bīja (Seed) mantras we bow down to You; to the form of the Slayer of Anger and Passion and in the form of Yai She is the Giver of Boons.

-10-

Vicce gives eternal freedom from fear, we bow to She who has the capacity to manifest in the form of mantras. Dhāṃ dhīṃ dhūṃ the wife of Śiva (literally the one with matted hair) Vāṃ vīṃ Vāgiśvarī (the Ruler of all Vibrations).

-11-

Krāṃ krīṃ krūṃ Oh Goddess who gives the key, Śrāṃ śrīṃ śrūṃ - She who is Peace in the gross body, Peace in the subtle body, Peace in the causal body be easily attained by me. In the form of the syllables Hūṃ hūṃ hūṃ, Jrāṃ jrīṃ Jrūṃ as the restrained sound of constant vibration emanating as a yawn from the junction of the eyes, ears, nose and throat.

-12-

Bhrāṃ bhrīṃ bhrūṃ to the Excellent Energy that is Extremely Fierce, to Bhairavi, the female Lord of Being, we bow, we bow to you.

Oṃ Aṃ Kaṃ Caṃ Taṃ Taṃ Paṃ Sāṃ
those who are intelligent, those who are intelligent
Devastate obstructions, devastate obstructions
Hrīṃ- Māyā, what can be perceived in the gross body, the subtle body, the causal body and beyond
Kṣāṃ - the perfect consciousness of the culmination
Kṣīṃ - the perfect culmination in the causal body
Śrīṃ - the perfection of peace in the subtle body and in the causal body
Give life, give life

Destroy angry speech, destroy angry speech
Illuminate, Illuminate
Erase, erase
Hūṃ - Cut the ego
Phaṭ - Purify
Jrāṃ - expansive, the perfect consciousness in the mind of all beings born
Ultimate purity
Aiṃ - Wisdom
Hrīṃ- Māyā, what can be perceived in the gross body, the subtle body, the causal body and beyond
Klīṃ- The cause of dissolving manifested existence in the perfection of the causal body
Make them pleasing, make them pleasing
Hang on, hang on
With the humming, humming (eternal vibration)
Binding, binding
Bhrāṃ bhrīṃ bhrūṃ
to the Excellent Energy that is Extremely Fierce, to Bhairavi, the female Lord Beyond Fear
Contracting, contracting (diminishing), angry speech, angry speech
Mlīṃ - The measurement of perfection from manifested existence to the causal body
Svāhā - I am One with God!

-13-

Pāṃ pīṃ pūṃ Pārvati, the wife of Śiva; the Potentiality of Nature is full and complete.
Khāṃ khīṃ khūṃ (the three stages of kecarī where one levitates) as a heavenly being we fly up into the atmosphere.
Mlāṃ mlīṃ mlūṃ - the measurement of perfection of manifested existence with Consciousness in the gross body, subtle body, and causal body
Given the purpose of the Song that gives the Key.

-14-

Do not give this to one who is not a devotee, oh Pārvati, protect the secret. Whoever will recite the seven Hundred Verses without the Song which gives the Key

-15-

will not be able to be victorious in attaining perfection; then it will be like crying in the forest.

Thus ends the Song which gives the Key explained by Īśvara to Pārvati in the Respected Dāmara Tantra.

Devipuṣpāñjalīstotram

The Song Which Offers Flower Petals to the Goddess

-1-

Whose Divine Play is this Universe, Who is worshiped by Nandi, the Attendant of Śiva. Who dwells at the apex of Vindhya, the best of mountains (Which is the personification of the Knowledge of Humility), Who is radiantly shining with the Consciousness that pervades all (Viṣṇu), and who is praised by the Triumphant One (Indra). Oh Supreme Goddess, the wife of the one with a blue throat (Śiva), Who is the head of the abundant (universal) family, Who created Abundance. Victory, Victory to you! Oh Slayer of the Great Ego, Oh One with beautiful braided hair, Oh Goddess of Inspiration (Daughter of the Mountains).

-2-

Who causes a rain of divine blessings, Who overpowered Irresistible Temptation, Who endured and forgave Foul Mouth, Who delights in Her own bliss. Who is the cause of Increase in the three worlds, who is satisfying to Śaṅkara, the Cause of Peace, Who forcibly takes away our faults, Who delights in cries of victory. Who removes the anger born of Duality and Who is angry with the Sons of Duality, Who removes illusion and arrogance, the daughter of the ocean (Lakṣmī). Victory, Victory to you! Oh Slayer of the Great Ego, Oh One with beautiful braided hair, Oh Goddess of Inspiration (Daughter of the Mountains).

-3-

Oh Mother of the perceivable universe, my own Mother, Who loves residing in the forest of Kadamba trees and delights in laughter and mirth, Who is the pinnacle of Crown Jewels, Whose abode is in the midst of lofty Himalayan Peaks. Who is as sweet as sweetness itself, who subdued the pride of Too Much and Too Little, the destroyer of Too Little, Who enjoys the Uproar of Noise. Victory, Victory to you! Oh Slayer of the Great Ego, Oh One with beautiful braided hair, Oh Goddess of Inspiration (Daughter of the Mountains).

-4-

Who with a single utterance of the mantra "Huṃ" (meaning cut the ego) reduced Sinful Eyes into a hundred bits of ash. Who in the battle with the thoughts completely dried up the Seed of Desire and the thoughts born from him which were like vines rising from seeds. Who offered Self-Conceit and Self-Deprecation as the great oblations to the Auspicious Consciousness of Infinite Goodness

(Śiva) thus satisfying and delighting the disembodied spirits attending him. Victory, Victory to you! Oh Slayer of the Great Ego, Oh One with beautiful braided hair, Oh Goddess of Inspiration (Daughter of the Mountains).

-5-

Oh one who cuts the demons into hundreds of pieces and severs the trunks from great battle elephants, whose great lion is skilled in valor and terrifyingly tears apart the enemies in the form of limitations to the soul. Who has cut into pieces the enemy generals with the strength of her own arms. Victory, Victory to you! Oh Slayer of the Great Ego, Oh One with beautiful braided hair, Oh Goddess of Inspiration (Daughter of the Mountains).

-6-

Who adorns Herself with ornaments dancing on Her shining arms following the movements of Her bow during each instant of the battle, Whose golden arrows become of reddish hue (with blood) when they strike the foolish Enemies and slay them, while they emit their loud howls and screams at the top of their voices. Who made the battlefield with the four fold army into a stage to present the drama with the screams of the soldiers. Victory, Victory to you! Oh Slayer of the Great Ego, Oh One with beautiful braided hair, Oh Goddess of Inspiration (Daughter of the Mountains).

-7-

Who Manifested to destroy the demons intoxicated with arrogance in their quest for war. Who possesses indefeatable and imperishable energy, Who made Lord Śiva Her messenger, that Siva who is distinguished by efficiency in thought, and is the Lord of ghosts and goblins, Who is honored for rejecting the proposal from the evil-minded and ignorant messenger from the demon Self-Conceit, and hence bringing an end to the demons themselves. Victory, Victory to you! Oh Slayer of the Great Ego, Oh One with beautiful braided hair, Oh Goddess of Inspiration (Daughter of the Mountains).

-8-

Who gave freedom from fear to the heroic enemy soldiers when their wives took refuge in Her, Who with trident in Her hands captured the Rulers of the Three Worlds who opposed Her. Whose Victory give rise to Dumi-Dumi sounds of the Dundubhi Drum flowing incessantly like water which fills all the directions with joy. Victory, Victory to you! Oh Slayer of the Great Ego, Oh One with beautiful braided hair, Oh Goddess of Inspiration (Daughter of the Mountains).

-9-

Following the rhythm of the Great Battle, the celestial dancers dance to the rhythms of Ta-Tha-Theyi, Ta-Theyi, expressing the sentiment of the battle with their dramatic movements. Following the rhythm of the Great Battle, the celestial musicians create music which captures the intensity of the battle with the Talas (musical beats) like Ku-Kutha, Ku-Kutha, Ga-Da-Dha, Ga-Da-Dha. Following the rhythm of the Great Battle a steady deep sound of Dhu-Dhu-Kuta, Dhu-Kuta, Dhim-Dhimi is played from the Mṛdaṅgam (a large drum) in the background. Victory, Victory to you! Oh Slayer of the Great Ego, Oh One with beautiful braided hair, Oh Goddess of Inspiration (Daughter of the Mountains).

-10-

Who is the continuous repetition of shouts of "Jaya Jaya, Victory, Victory!" Who is the resounding sound of "Jaya" at the time of victory, The supreme song of praise, Who is worshipped in the universe as that which is Beyond. The tinkling sound of Her anklets captivates even the Lord of Beings, Who acts as half of the Cosmic Dancer, who is both male and female, who leads the Universal Play, delighting in the excellent song (of the Cosmic Sound "Oṃ"). Victory, Victory to you! Oh Slayer of the Great Ego, Oh One with beautiful braided hair, Oh Goddess of Inspiration (Daughter of the Mountains).

-11-

Who is benevolent, gracious, favorable and pleasant, Who is the captivating union of the excellent mind with beauty enhanced by love, Who makes the night subservient, Who is the Dark One within the night, Who is the night of the night, Whose face is surrounded by rays of moon light, Whose excellent eyes are distinguished amongst the swarm of beautiful black bees as the supreme Queens of black bees. Victory, Victory to you! Oh Slayer of the Great Ego, Oh One with beautiful braided hair, Oh Goddess of Inspiration (Daughter of the Mountains).

-12-

Who is accompanied in the Great Battle against excellent warriors by young girls who appear to be as tender as creepers of jasmine, yet fighting against the enemies. Whose is accompanied by girls from the Bheel Tribe, who are tender like creepers of jasmine and make a buzzing sound like swarms of bees. Upon Whose face is a smile of joy, which appears with a red color like the shining forth of the dawn, or the blossoming of excellent buds of flowers. Victory, Victory to you! Oh Slayer of the Great Ego, Oh One with beautiful braided hair, Oh Goddess of Inspiration (Daughter of the Mountains).

-13-

Who is like an intoxicated royal elephant from whose cheeks the thick Mada (Intoxicant) oozes out and falls incessantly. Who is the Daughter of the King and from Whom come the Treasures of arts, beauty and energy, which are ornaments of the three worlds. Who is like the Daughter of the God of Love who gives rise to the desires and infatuation in the mind for women with a beautiful smile. Victory, Victory to you! Oh Slayer of the Great Ego, Oh One with beautiful braided hair, Oh Goddess of Inspiration (Daughter of the Mountains).

-14-

On whose forehead are the spotlessly pure petals of the lotus and the pure shining symbol of the Light of Devotion (the moon), charming like beauty enhanced by love, Who is completely shining and moves with the playful, soft movements of a flock of swans, proceeding like the moon in its own abode. Whose ornamented and braided hair is beautiful and sweet like a swarm of bees amongst a circle of blue lotuses, as well as bakula flowers covered with bees. Victory, Victory to you! Oh Slayer of the Great Ego, Oh One with beautiful braided hair, Oh Goddess of Inspiration (Daughter of the Mountains).

-15-

Who makes the sound of the flute in Her hands appear so sweet as to put the Cuckoo who sings with such beauty to shame. Whose enchanting songs along with the tribal girls, while they walk in the mountain groves, which are brightly colored due to the blooming flowers. Who plays with the tribal women of Her group who are filled with good qualities. Victory, Victory to you! Oh Slayer of the Great Ego, Oh One with beautiful braided hair, Oh Goddess of Inspiration (Daughter of the Mountains).

-16-

Whose waist is adorned with silk clothes of various colors, the luster of which eclipses the brightness of the Moon. Whose toe-nails shine reflecting the radiance of the gems from the crowns of the Gods and Asuras who are bowing to Her feet. Whose abundant breasts are swollen like the peaks of the golden mountains. Victory,

Victory to you! Oh Slayer of the Great Ego, Oh One with beautiful braided hair, Oh Goddess of Inspiration (Daughter of the Mountains).

-17-

Who conquers thousands of enemies who fight against Her with thousands of hands. Who Herself manifests a thousand hands, and Who is praised by thousands of devotees with thousands of hands for creating the Leader of the Gods (Her son Kārttikeya) to fight with the Demon Tārakāsura (the Illuminator of Duality). Who is pleased with both the devotion of King Suratha for worldly gains, and also the excellent devotion of the businessman Samādhi, who desired Spiritual Knowledge. Victory, Victory to you! Oh Slayer of the Great Ego, Oh One with beautiful braided hair, Oh Goddess of Inspiration (Daughter of the Mountains).

-18-

Oh Benevolent Goddess accompanied by Lord Śiva, whoever serves Your highly auspicious lotus feet everyday, which are the abode of compassion, serves the feet of Lakṣmī, will he not become filled with purity and prosperity? Therefore, how can I not practice devotion towards those feet, Oh Auspicious Mother? Victory, Victory to you! Oh Slayer of the Great Ego, Oh One with beautiful braided hair, Oh Goddess of Inspiration (Daughter of the Mountains).

-19-

When someone offers You waters for Your bath, shining like gold in the early morning sun, he will experience such happiness, like Indra embracing His wife Śachī in heaven. I take refuge at Your feet, Oh Vāni (Goddess Saraswatī), and I Prostate before You, in Whom resides All Auspiciousness. Victory, Victory to you! Oh Slayer of the Great Ego, Oh One with beautiful braided hair, Oh Goddess of Inspiration (Daughter of the Mountains).

-20-

Whose moon-like face is the abode of spotless and stainless purity which certainly subdues all impurities. Therefore my mind has turned away from worldly attraction, like the Apsaras present in Indra's heaven. Without Your Grace, how is it possible to discover the treasure of Śiva's Name within us? Victory, Victory to you! Oh Slayer of the Great Ego, Oh One with beautiful braided hair, Oh Goddess of Inspiration (Daughter of the Mountains).

-21-

Oh Umā, You must bestow Your grace on those who are lowly like me, as You are our Compassionate Mother. Oh Mother of the Universe, You shower Your grace on us, and in the same manner, You fire Your arrows (to protect us). Oh Supreme Goddess, please do whatever is appropriate in this circumstance to drive away my pain and difficulties. Victory, Victory to you! Oh Slayer of the Great Ego, Oh One with beautiful braided hair, Oh Goddess of Inspiration (Daughter of the Mountains).

-22-

This song of praise makes one pure through intense meditation, whether recited with discipline or without, and the Supreme Goddess Lakṣmī will become the servant of those who worship.

Thus is the completion of the Song which offers flower petals to the Goddess.

Bīja Mantras – English Translations

तन्त्ररूपं रात्रिसूक्तम्

tantrarūpaṃ rātrisūktam

Tantrik Form of the Praise to the Night of Duality

1	ब्लूं	blūṃ	The protection of perfect strength in manifested existence
2	ठां	ṭhāṃ	The consciousness of the perfect supremacy of the great teacher
3	ह्रीं	hrīṃ	All of Maya: that which can be perceived in the gross body, the subtle body, known through intuition and beyond
4	स्त्रां	strāṃ	The consciousness of the perfect knowledge of tat twam asi in the subtle body
5	स्लूं	slūṃ	The protection of the perfect knowledge in manifestation
6	क्रैं	kraiṃ	The cause of perfect wisdom in the mind
7	त्रां	trāṃ	The consciousness of the perfection of tat twam asi in the mind
8	फ्रां	phrāṃ	The consciousness of the fruit of perfect karma in the mind
9	जीं	jīṃ	The perfection of all beings born in the causal body
10	लूं	lūṃ	The protection of perfection in manifested existence
11	स्लूं	slūṃ	The protection of the perfect knowledge in manifestation
12	नों	noṃ	The consciousness of the subtle sound of manifested existence
13	स्त्रीं	strīṃ	The perfection of the knowledge of tat twam asi in the subtle and causal bodies
14	प्रूं	prūṃ	The protection of perfect purity in the mind
15	स्रूं	srūṃ	The protection of perfect knowledge in the mind
16	जां	jāṃ	The perfection of consciousness in all beings born
17	वौं	vauṃ	The perfection of divine vibrations
18	ओं	oṃ	The divine energy of the subtle sound of existence

प्रथमोऽध्यायः

prathamo-dhyāyaḥ
Chapter One

	ॐ	oṃ	The infinite beyond conception
	ऐं	aiṃ	The ultimate wisdom
1	श्रीं	śrīṃ	The perfection of peace in the mind and heart
2	ह्रीं	hrīṃ	All of Maya: that which can be perceived in the gross body, the subtle body, known through intuition and beyond
3	क्लीं	klīṃ	The cause of manifested existence merging into the causal body in perfection
4	श्रीं	śrīṃ	The perfection of peace in the mind and heart
5	प्रीं	prīṃ	The purity of the mind merging into the causal body in perfection
6	ह्रां	hrāṃ	The perfect consciousness in the gross and subtle bodies
7	ह्रीं	hrīṃ	All of Maya: that which can be perceived in the gross body, the subtle body, known through intuition and beyond
8	सौं	sauṃ	The perfection of divine knowledge
9	प्रें	preṃ	The perfect pure vibrations in the mind
10	म्रीं	mrīṃ	The measurement of perfection in the subtle and causal bodies
11	ह्लीं	hlīṃ	The manifestation of perfection in the gross and causal bodies
12	म्लीं	mlīṃ	The measurement of perfection from manifested existence to the causal body
13	स्त्रीं	strīṃ	The perfection of the knowledge of tat twam asi in the subtle and causal bodies
14	क्रां	krāṃ	The perfect consciousness of the primary cause of existence in the subtle body
15	ह्स्लीं	hslīṃ	The perfection of knowledge from manifested existence to the causal body
16	क्रीं	krīṃ	The cause of the subtle body merging into the causal body in perfection
17	चां	cāṃ	The perfect manifestation of consciousness
18	में	meṃ	The measurement of the perfection of vibrations

19	क्रीं	krīṃ	The cause of the subtle body merging into the causal body in perfection
20	वैं	vaiṃ	The vibrations of the perfection of the energy of wisdom
21	ह्रौं	hrauṃ	The perfect manifestation of the supreme divinity in the gross and subtle bodies
22	युं	yuṃ	The control of all circumstances for the ultimate perfection
23	जुं	juṃ	The perfection of the birth of all circumstances
24	हं	haṃ	The manifestation of divinity in perceivable form
25	शं	śaṃ	The perfection of peace
26	रौं	rauṃ	The divinity manifest in perfection in the subtle body
27	यं	yaṃ	The perfection of control
28	विं	viṃ	The vibrations of perfect knowledge
29	वैं	vaiṃ	The vibrations of perfect wisdom
30	चें	ceṃ	The vibrations of perfect consciousness
31	ह्रीं	hrīṃ	All of Maya: that which can be perceived in the gross body, the subtle body, known through intuition and beyond
32	क्रं	kraṃ	The cause of the perfection in the subtle body
33	सं	saṃ	The manifestation of perfect knowledge
34	कं	kaṃ	The cause of the perfect beginning
35	श्रीं	śrīṃ	The perfection of peace in the mind and heart
36	त्रौं	trauṃ	The divinity of the perfection of tat twam asi in the mind
37	स्त्रां	strāṃ	The consciousness of the perfect knowledge of tat twam asi in the subtle body
38	ज्यैं	jyaiṃ	The perfect control with wisdom for all beings born
39	रौं	rauṃ	The divinity manifest in perfection in the subtle body
40	द्रां	drāṃ	The perfect perception of consciousness in the mind
41	द्रों	droṃ	The perfect perception with full and complete consciousness in God

42	ह्रां	hrāṃ	The perfect consciousness in the gross and subtle bodies
43	द्रूं	drūṃ	The protection of perfect perception in the mind
44	शां	śāṃ	The consciousness of perfect peace
45	मीं	mīṃ	The perfect measurement of the causal body
46	श्रौं	śrauṃ	The perfection of divine peace in the mind
47	जुं	juṃ	The perfection of the birth of all circumstances
48	ह्लूं	hlrūṃ	The perfect protection in the gross and subtle bodies of manifested existence
49	श्रूं	śrūṃ	The protection of perfect peace in the mind
50	प्रीं	prīṃ	The purity of the mind merging into the causal body in perfection
51	रं	raṃ	The perfection in the subtle body
52	वं	vaṃ	The perfection of all vibrations
53	ब्रीं	brīṃ	The cause of perfect strength in the mind
54	ब्लं	blaṃ	The perfection of strength in manifested existence
55	स्रौं	strauṃ	The perfection of the divine knowledge of tat twam asi in the mind
56	ल्वां	lvāṃ	The consciousness of perfect vibrations in manifested existence
57	लूं	lūṃ	The protection of perfection in manifested existence
58	सां	sāṃ	The consciousness of perfect knowledge.
59	रौं	rauṃ	The divinity manifest in perfection in the subtle body
60	स्हौं	shauṃ	The perfect divine knowledge that pervades the gross body of existence
61	कुं	kuṃ	The cause of the perfect circumstance
62	शौं	śauṃ	The perfection of divine peace
63	श्रौं	śrauṃ	The perfection of divine peace in the mind
64	वं	vaṃ	The perfection of all vibrations

65	त्रूं	trūṃ	The protection of the perfection of tat twam asi in the mind
66	क्रौं	krauṃ	The perfect illumination of the divine cause in the subtle body
67	क्लं	klaṃ	The cause of perfection in manifested existence
68	क्लीं	klīṃ	The cause of manifested existence merging into the causal body in perfection
69	श्रीं	śrīṃ	The perfection of peace in the mind and heart
70	ब्लूं	blūṃ	The protection of perfect strength in manifested existence
71	ठां	ṭhāṃ	The consciousness of the perfect supremacy of the great teacher
72	ह्रीं	hrīṃ	All of Maya: that which can be perceived in the gross body, the subtle body, known through intuition and beyond
73	स्त्रां	strāṃ	The consciousness of the perfect knowledge of tat twam asi in the subtle body
74	स्लूं	slūṃ	The protection of the perfect knowledge in manifestation
75	क्रैं	kraiṃ	The cause of perfect wisdom in the mind
76	त्रां	trāṃ	The consciousness of the perfection of tat twam asi in the mind
77	फ्रां	phrāṃ	The consciousness of the fruit of perfect karma in the mind
78	जीं	jīṃ	The perfection of all beings born in the causal body
79	लूं	lūṃ	The protection of perfection in manifested existence
80	स्लूं	slūṃ	The protection of the perfect knowledge in manifestation
81	नों	noṃ	The consciousness of the subtle sound of manifested existence
82	स्त्रीं	strīṃ	The perfection of the knowledge of tat twam asi in the subtle and causal bodies
83	प्रूं	prūṃ	The protection of perfect purity in the mind
84	सूं	sūṃ	The protection of the perfect knowledge
85	ज्रां	jrāṃ	The perfect understanding of the minds of all living beings
86	वौं	vauṃ	The perfection of divine vibrations
87	ओं	oṃ	The divine energy of the subtle sound of existence

88	श्रौं	śrauṃ	The perfection of divine peace in the mind
89	ऋं	ṛṃ	The perfect attitude of a seer of divine inspiration
90	रूं	rūṃ	The protection of the perfect mind
91	क्लीं	klīṃ	The cause of manifested existence merging into the causal body in perfection
92	दुं	duṃ	The perfect perception of all circumstances
93	ह्रीं	hrīṃ	All of Maya: that which can be perceived in the gross body, the subtle body, known through intuition and beyond
94	गूं	gūṃ	The protection of the supreme lord of wisdom who removes all obstacles
95	लां	lāṃ	The perfect manifestation of consciousness
96	ह्रां	hrāṃ	The perfect consciousness in the gross and subtle bodies
97	गं	gaṃ	The supreme lord of wisdom who removes all obstacles
98	ऐं	aiṃ	The ultimate wisdom
99	श्रौं	śrauṃ	The perfection of divine peace in the mind
100	जूं	jūṃ	The protection of perfection in all beings born
101	डें	ḍeṃ	The perfect vibrations of worship with excessive devotion
102	श्रौं	śrauṃ	The perfection of divine peace in the mind
103	छां	chāṃ	The consciousness of the reflection of perfection
104	क्लीं	klīṃ	The cause of manifested existence merging into perfection in the causal body

द्वितीयोऽध्यायः

dvitīyo-dhyāyaḥ

Chapter Two

1	श्रौं	śrauṃ	The perfection of divine peace in the mind
2	श्रीं	śrīṃ	The perfection of peace in the mind and heart
3	ह्सूं	hsūṃ	The protection of perfect knowledge in the gross body
4	हौं	hauṃ	The perfect divinity in the gross body
5	ह्रीं	hrīṃ	All of Maya: that which can be perceived in the gross body, the subtle body, known through intuition and beyond
6	अं	aṃ	The commencement of creation
7	क्लीं	klīṃ	The cause of manifested existence merging into the causal body in perfection
8	चां	cāṃ	The perfect manifestation of consciousness
9	मुं	muṃ	The measurement of the circumstances of perfection
10	डां	ḍāṃ	The perfect consciousness of worship with excessive devotion
11	यैं	yaiṃ	The perfect control with wisdom
12	विं	viṃ	The vibrations of perfect knowledge
13	च्चें	cceṃ	The perfection of union between consciousness and wisdom
14	ईं	īṃ	The cause of perfection
15	सौं	sauṃ	The perfection of divine knowledge
16	व्रां	vrāṃ	The perfect consciousness of vibrations in the mind
17	त्रौं	trauṃ	The divinity of the perfection of tat twam asi in the mind
18	लूं	lūṃ	The protection of perfection in manifested existence
19	वं	vaṃ	The perfection of all vibrations
20	ह्रां	hrāṃ	The perfect consciousness in the gross and subtle bodies

21	क्रीं	krīṃ	The cause of the subtle body merging into the causal body in perfection
22	सौं	sauṃ	The perfection of divine knowledge
23	यं	yaṃ	The perfection of control
24	ऐं	aiṃ	The ultimate wisdom
25	मूं	mūṃ	The protection of the measurement of perfection
26	सः	saḥ	The perfect knowledge of name and form
27	हं	haṃ	The manifestation of divinity in perceivable form
28	सं	saṃ	The manifestation of perfect knowledge
29	सों	soṃ	The manifestation of perfect divine knowledge
30	शं	śaṃ	The perfection of peace
31	हं	haṃ	The manifestation of divinity in perceivable form
32	ह्रौं	hrauṃ	The perfect manifestation of the supreme divinity in the gross and subtle bodies
33	म्लीं	mlīṃ	The measurement of perfection from manifested existence to the causal body
34	यूं	yūṃ	The protection of the perfect control
35	त्रूं	trūṃ	The protection of the perfection of tat twam asi in the mind
36	स्रीं	srīṃ	The perfect knowledge in the mind and heart
37	आं	āṃ	The perfect consciousness
38	प्रें	preṃ	The perfect pure vibrations in the mind
39	शं	śaṃ	The perfection of peace
40	ह्रां	hrāṃ	The perfect consciousness in the gross and subtle bodies
41	स्मूं	smūṃ	The protection of the measurement of perfect knowledge
42	ऊं	ūṃ	The perfect protection
43	गूं	gūṃ	The perfect protection of the supreme lord of wisdom who removes all obstacles

44	व्यं	vyaṃ	The perfect control of vibrations
45	ह्रं	hraṃ	The perfect manifestation in the gross and subtle bodies
46	भैं	bhaiṃ	The perfection of the attitude of wisdom
47	ह्रां	hrāṃ	The perfect consciousness in the gross and subtle bodies
48	क्रूं	krūṃ	The protection of the cause of perfection in the subtle body
49	मूं	mūṃ	The protection of the measurement of perfection
50	ल्रीं	lrīṃ	The manifestation of perfection in the subtle and causal bodies
51	श्रां	śrāṃ	The consciousness of perfect peace in the mind
52	द्रूं	drūṃ	The protection of perfect perception in the mind
53	ह्रूं	hrūṃ	The protection of perfection in the gross and subtle bodies
54	ह्सौं	hsauṃ	The manifestation of divine knowledge in the gross body
55	क्रां	krāṃ	The perfect consciousness of the primary cause of existence in the subtle body
56	स्हौं	shauṃ	The perfect divine knowledge that pervades the gross body of existence
57	म्लूं	mlūṃ	The protection of the perfect measurement of manifested existence
58	श्रीं	śrīṃ	The perfection of peace in the mind and heart
59	गैं	gaiṃ	The perfect wisdom of the supreme lord of wisdom who removes all obstacles
60	क्रीं	krīṃ	The cause of the subtle body merging into the causal body in perfection
61	त्रीं	trīṃ	The manifestation of the perfection of tat twam asi in the mind and heart
62	क्सीं	ksīṃ	The cause of the perfection of divine knowledge in the causal body
63	फ्रां	phrāṃ	The consciousness of the fruit of perfect karma in the mind
64	फ्रैं	phraiṃ	The perfection of the fruit of wisdom of karma in the mind
65	ह्रीं	hrīṃ	All of Maya: that which can be perceived in the gross body, the subtle body, known through intuition and beyond
66	शां	śāṃ	The consciousness of perfect peace

67	क्ष्म्रीं	kṣmrīṃ	The measurement of the culmination of perfection in the mind and heart
68	रौं	rauṃ	The divinity manifest in perfection in the subtle body
69	ङूं	ṅūṃ	The protection of that which causes the end to duality

तृतीयोऽध्यायः

tṛtīyo-dhyāyaḥ

Chapter Three

1	श्रौं	śrauṃ	The perfection of divine peace in the mind
2	क्लीं	klīṃ	The cause of manifested existence merging into the causal body in perfection
3	सां	sāṃ	The consciousness of perfect knowledge
4	त्रों	troṃ	The manifestation of the perfection of tat twam asi in the subtle body
5	प्रूं	prūṃ	The protection of perfect purity in the mind
6	ग्लौं	glauṃ	The divine manifestation of the supreme lord of wisdom who removes all obstacles
7	क्रौं	krauṃ	The perfect illumination of the divine cause in the subtle body
8	व्रीं	vrīṃ	The perfection of vibrations in the mind and heart
9	स्लीं	slīṃ	The knowledge of the perfect union of manifested existence with the causal body
10	ह्रीं	hrīṃ	All of Maya: that which can be perceived in the gross body, the subtle body, known through intuition and beyond
11	हौं	hauṃ	The perfect divinity in the gross body
12	श्रां	śrāṃ	The consciousness of perfect peace in the mind
13	ग्रीं	grīṃ	The perfect manifestation of the supreme lord of wisdom in the mind and heart
14	क्रूं	krūṃ	The protection of the cause of perfection in the subtle body
15	क्रीं	krīṃ	The cause of the subtle body merging into the causal body in perfection
16	यां	yāṃ	The consciousness of perfect control
17	द्लूं	dlūṃ	The protection of the perception of the perfect manifested existence
18	द्रूं	drūṃ	The protection of perfect perception in the mind
19	क्षं	kṣaṃ	The completion of the pilgrimage in perfection
20	ओं	oṃ	The divine energy of the subtle sound of existence

21	क्रौं	kraum̩	The perfect illumination of the divine cause in the subtle body
22	क्ष्म्क्लृीं	kṣmklrīṃ	The cause of the perfect measurement from beginning to end
23	वां	vāṃ	The consciousness of the perfection of vibrations
24	श्रूं	śrūṃ	The protection of perfect peace in the mind
25	ग्लूं	glūṃ	The protection of the manifestation of the supreme lord of wisdom who removes all obstacles
26	ल्रीं	lrīṃ	The manifestation of perfection in the subtle and causal bodies
27	प्रें	preṃ	The perfect pure vibrations in the mind
28	हूं	hūṃ	The protection of the cutting of the ego
29	ह्रौं	hrauṃ	The perfect manifestation of the supreme divinity in the gross and subtle bodies
30	दें	deṃ	The perception of the vibrations of perfection
31	नूं	nūṃ	The protection of perfect consciousness
32	आं	āṃ	The perfect consciousness
33	फ्रां	phrāṃ	The consciousness of the fruit of perfect karma in the mind
34	प्रीं	prīṃ	The purity of the mind merging into the causal body in perfection
35	दं	daṃ	The perception of perfection
36	फ्रीं	phrīṃ	The perfection of the fruit of karma in the mind and heart
37	ह्रीं	hrīṃ	All of Maya: that which can be perceived in the gross body, the subtle body, known through intuition and beyond
38	गूं	gūṃ	The protection of the supreme lord of wisdom who removes all obstacles
39	श्रौं	śrauṃ	The perfection of divine peace in the mind
40	सां	sāṃ	The consciousness of perfect knowledge.
41	श्रीं	śrīṃ	The perfection of peace in the mind and heart

42	जुं	juṃ	The perfection of the birth of all circumstances
43	हं	haṃ	The manifestation of divinity in perceivable form
44	सं	saṃ	The manifestation of perfect knowledge

चतुर्थोऽध्यायः

caturtho-dhyāyaḥ

Chapter Four

1	श्रौं	śrauṃ	The perfection of divine peace in the mind
2	सौं	sauṃ	The perfection of divine knowledge
3	दीं	dīṃ	The perfect perception in the causal body
4	प्रें	preṃ	The perfect pure vibrations in the mind
5	यां	yāṃ	The consciousness of perfect control
6	रूं	rūṃ	The perfect protection of the mind
7	मं	maṃ	The measurement of perfection
8	सूं	sūṃ	The protection of the perfect knowledge
9	श्रां	śrāṃ	The consciousness of perfect peace in the mind
10	औं	auṃ	The perfect divinity of all the threes
11	लूं	lūṃ	The protection of perfection in manifested existence
12	डूं	ḍūṃ	The protection of the perfect love for Divine Mother with excessive devotion
13	जूं	jūṃ	The protection of perfection in all beings born
14	धूं	dhūṃ	The protection of the perfect meditation
15	त्रें	treṃ	The vibrations of the perfection of tat twam asi in the mind
16	ह्रीं	hrīṃ	All of Maya: that which can be perceived in the gross body, the subtle body, known through intuition and beyond
17	श्रीं	śrīṃ	The perfection of peace in the mind and heart
18	ईं	īṃ	The cause of perfection
19	ह्रां	hrāṃ	The perfect consciousness in the gross and subtle bodies
20	ह्लूं	hlrūṃ	The perfect protection in the gross and subtle bodies of manifested existence

21	क्लूं	klūṃ	The cause of the protection of perfection in manifested existence
22	क्रां	krāṃ	The perfect consciousness of the primary cause of existence in the subtle body
23	ल्लूं	llūṃ	The protection of perfection in the gross body of manifested existence
24	फ्रें	phreṃ	The perfect wisdom of the fruit of karma in the mind
25	क्रीं	krīṃ	The cause of the subtle body merging into the causal body in perfection
26	म्लूं	mlūṃ	The protection of the perfect measurement of manifested existence
27	घ्रें	ghreṃ	The vibrations which remove fear from the mind
28	श्रौं	śrauṃ	The perfection of divine peace in the mind
29	ह्रौं	hrauṃ	The perfect manifestation of the supreme divinity in the gross and subtle bodies
30	व्रीं	vrīṃ	The perfection of vibrations in the mind and heart
31	ह्रीं	hrīṃ	All of Maya: that which can be perceived in the gross body, the subtle body, known through intuition and beyond
32	त्रौं	trauṃ	The divinity of the perfection of tat twam asi in the mind
33	हल्लौं	hllauṃ	The divine perfection which permeates the gross body of manifested existence
34	गीं	gīṃ	The perfection in the heart of the supreme lord of wisdom who removes all obstacles
35	यूं	yūṃ	The protection of perfect control
36	ह्लीं	hlīṃ	The manifestation of perfection in the gross and causal bodies
37	ह्लूं	hlūṃ	The protection of the manifestation of perfection in the gross body
38	श्रौं	śrauṃ	The perfection of divine peace in the mind
39	ओं	oṃ	The divine energy of the subtle sound of existence
40	अं	aṃ	The commencement of creation
41	म्हौं	mhauṃ	The measurement of perfect divinity in the gross body
42	प्रीं	prīṃ	The purity of the mind merging into the causal body in perfection

पञ्चमोऽध्यायः

pañcamo-dhyāyaḥ

Chapter Five

1	श्रौं	śrauṃ	The perfection of divine peace in the mind
2	प्रीं	prīṃ	The purity of the mind merging into the causal body in perfection
3	ओं	oṃ	The divine energy of the subtle sound of existence
4	ह्रीं	hrīṃ	All of Maya: that which can be perceived in the gross body, the subtle body, known through intuition and beyond
5	ल्रीं	lrīṃ	The manifestation of perfection in the subtle and causal bodies
6	त्रों	troṃ	The manifestation of the perfection of tat twam asi in the subtle body
7	क्रीं	krīṃ	The cause of the subtle body merging into the causal body in perfection
8	ह्सौं	hsauṃ	The manifestation of divine knowledge in the gross body
9	ह्रीं	hrīṃ	All of Maya: that which can be perceived in the gross body, the subtle body, known through intuition and beyond
10	श्रीं	śrīṃ	The perfection of peace in the mind and heart
11	हूं	hūṃ	The protection of the cutting of the ego
12	क्लीं	klīṃ	The cause of manifested existence merging into the causal body in perfection
13	रौं	rauṃ	The divinity manifest in perfection in the subtle body
14	स्त्रीं	strīṃ	The perfection of the knowledge of tat twam asi in the subtle and causal bodies
15	म्लीं	mlīṃ	The measurement of perfection from manifested existence to the causal body
16	प्लूं	plūṃ	The protection of the perfect purity in manifested existence
17	स्हौं	shauṃ	The perfect divine knowledge that pervades the gross body of existence
18	स्त्रीं	strīṃ	The perfection of the knowledge of tat twam asi in the subtle and causal bodies
19	ग्लूं	glūṃ	The protection of the supreme lord of wisdom who removes all obstacles
20	व्रीं	vrīṃ	The perfection of vibrations in the mind and heart

21	सौं	sauṃ	The perfection of divine knowledge
22	लूं	lūṃ	The protection of perfection in manifested existence
23	ल्लूं	llūṃ	The protection of perfection in the gross body of manifested existence
24	द्रां	drāṃ	The perfect perception of consciousness in the mind
25	क्सां	ksāṃ	The cause of the perfection of the consciousness of divine knowledge
26	क्ष्म्रीं	kṣmrīṃ	The measurement of the culmination of perfection in the mind and heart
27	ग्लौं	glauṃ	The divine manifestation of the supreme lord of wisdom who removes all obstacles
28	स्कं	skaṃ	The knowledge of the perfect beginning
29	बूं	būṃ	The protection of perfect strength
30	स्क्लूं	sklūṃ	The knowledge which causes the protection of perfection in manifested existence
31	क्रौं	krauṃ	The perfect illumination of the divine cause in the subtle body
32	छ्रीं	chrīṃ	The perfect reflection in the mind and heart
33	म्लूं	mlūṃ	The protection of the perfect measurement of manifested existence
34	क्लूं	klūṃ	The cause of the protection of perfection in manifested existence
35	शां	śāṃ	The consciousness of perfect peace
36	ल्हीं	lhīṃ	The manifestation of perfection in the gross and causal bodies
37	स्रूं	srūṃ	The protection of perfect knowledge in the mind
38	ल्लीं	llīṃ	The perfect manifestation in the gross and causal bodies
39	लीं	līṃ	The perfect manifestation in the causal body
40	सं	saṃ	The manifestation of perfect knowledge
41	लूं	lūṃ	The protection of perfection in manifested existence
42	ह्सूं	hsūṃ	The protection of perfect knowledge in the gross body
43	श्रूं	śrūṃ	The protection of perfect peace in the mind

44	जूं	jūṃ	The protection of perfection in all beings born
45	ह्स्ल्रीं	hslrīṃ	The perfect knowledge which manifests in the gross, subtle and causal bodies of manifested existence
46	स्कीं	skīṃ	The cause of perfect knowledge in the causal body
47	क्लां	klāṃ	The cause of the perfect consciousness in manifested existence
48	श्रूं	śrūṃ	The protection of perfect peace in the mind
49	हं	haṃ	The manifestation of divinity in perceivable form
50	ह्लीं	hlīṃ	The manifestation of perfection in the gross and causal bodies
51	क्स्रूं	ksrūṃ	The cause of protection of perfect knowledge in the mind
52	द्रौं	drauṃ	The perfect perception of the divine mind
53	क्लूं	klūṃ	The cause of the protection of perfection in manifested existence
54	गां	gāṃ	The perfect consciousness of the supreme lord of wisdom who removes all obstacles
55	सं	saṃ	The manifestation of perfect knowledge
56	ल्स्रां	lsrāṃ	The perfect knowledge which makes consciousness manifest in the mind
57	फ्रीं	phrīṃ	The perfection of the fruit of karma in the mind and heart
58	स्लां	slāṃ	The knowledge of the perfect consciousness in manifested existence
59	ल्लूं	llūṃ	The protection of perfection in the gross body of manifested existence
60	फ्रें	phreṃ	The perfect wisdom of the fruit of karma in the mind
61	ओं	oṃ	The divine energy of the subtle sound of existence
62	स्म्लीं	smlīṃ	The perfect knowledge of the measurement from manifested existence to the causal body
63	ह्रां	hrāṃ	The perfect consciousness in the gross and subtle bodies
64	ॐ	oṃ	The infinite beyond conception
65	ह्लूं	hlūṃ	The protection of the manifestation of perfection in the gross body
66	हूं	hūṃ	The protection of the cutting of the ego

67	नं	naṃ	The manifestation of the perfect embodiment of consciousness
68	स्त्रां	srāṃ	The knowledge of perfect consciousness in the mind
69	वं	vaṃ	The perfection of all vibrations
70	मं	maṃ	The measurement of perfection
71	म्व्लीं	mvlīṃ	The measurement of the perfect vibrations from manifested existence to the causal body
72	शां	śāṃ	The consciousness of perfect peace
73	लं	laṃ	The perfection of manifested existence
74	भैं	bhaiṃ	The perfection of the attitude of wisdom
75	ल्लूं	llūṃ	The protection of perfection in the gross body of manifested existence
76	हौं	hauṃ	The perfect divinity in the gross body
77	ईं	īṃ	The cause of perfection
78	चें	ceṃ	The vibrations of perfect consciousness
79	ल्क्रीं	lkrīṃ	The manifested cause of perfection in the mind and the heart
80	ह्ल्रीं	hlrīṃ	The manifestation of perfection in the gross, subtle and causal bodies
81	क्ष्म्ल्रीं	kṣmlrīṃ	The culmination of the measurement of the manifestation of perfection in the gross, subtle and causal bodies
82	पूं	pūṃ	The protection of perfect purity
83	श्रौं	śrauṃ	The perfection of divine peace in the mind
84	ह्रौं	hrauṃ	The perfect manifestation of the supreme divinity in the gross and subtle bodies
85	भ्रूं	bhrūṃ	The protection of the perfect attitudes of the mind
86	क्स्त्रीं	kstrīṃ	The cause of the knowledge of tat twam asi in the mind and heart
87	आं	āṃ	The perfect consciousness
88	क्रूं	krūṃ	The protection of the cause of perfection in the subtle body
89	त्रूं	trūṃ	The protection of the perfection of tat twam asi in the mind

90	डुं	ḍuṃ	The circumstance of perfect devotion to the Divine Mother
91	जां	jāṃ	The perfection of consciousness in all beings born
92	ह्लूं	hlrūṃ	The perfect protection in the gross and subtle bodies of manifested existence
93	फ्रौं	phrauṃ	The perfect divinity of the fruit of karma in the mind
94	क्रौं	krauṃ	The perfect illumination of the divine cause in the subtle body
95	किं	kiṃ	The cause of perfection of the full and complete meaning
96	ग्लूं	glūṃ	The protection of the manifestation of the supreme lord of wisdom who removes all obstacles
97	छ्रक्लीं	chrklīṃ	The cause of the perfect appearance of the gross, subtle and causal bodies
98	रं	raṃ	The perfection in the subtle body
99	क्सैं	ksaiṃ	The cause of perfect knowledge which yields wisdom
100	स्हुं	shuṃ	The knowledge that brings perfection to the circumstances of the gross body
101	श्रौं	śrauṃ	The perfection of divine peace in the mind
102	श्श्रीं	śrśrīṃ	The perfection of more peace in your mind and heart
103	ओं	oṃ	The divine energy of the subtle sound of existence
104	लूं	lūṃ	The protection of perfection in manifested existence
105	ल्हूं	lhūṃ	The protection of perfection in the gross body of manifested existence
106	ल्लूं	llūṃ	The protection of perfection in the gross body of manifested existence
107	स्क्रीं	skrīṃ	The knowledge which causes perfection in the mind and heart
108	स्स्त्रौं	sstrauṃ	The various forms of knowledge of the perfection of the divinity of tat twam asi in the mind
109	स्भ्रूं	sbhrūṃ	The protection of the knowledge of the perfect attitudes of the mind
110	क्ष्मक्लीं	kṣmklīṃ	The measurement of the cause of perfection from manifested existence to the causal body from beginning to end
111	व्रीं	vrīṃ	The perfection of vibrations in the mind and heart

112	सीं	sīṃ	The perfection of divine knowledge in the causal body
113	भूं	bhūṃ	The protection of the perfect attitude
114	लां	lāṃ	The perfect manifestation of consciousness
115	श्रौं	śrauṃ	The perfection of divine peace in the mind
116	स्हैं	shaiṃ	The knowledge of the perfection of wisdom in the gross body
117	ह्रीं	hrīṃ	All of Maya: that which can be perceived in the gross body, the subtle body, known through intuition and beyond
118	श्रीं	śrīṃ	The perfection of peace in the mind and heart
119	फ्रें	phreṃ	The perfect wisdom of the fruit of karma in the mind
120	रूं	rūṃ	The protection of the perfect mind
121	च्छ्रूं	cchrūṃ	The protection of the perfect appearance of consciousness in the subtle body
122	ल्हूं	lhūṃ	The protection of perfection in the gross body of manifested existence
123	कं	kaṃ	The cause of the perfect beginning
124	द्रें	dreṃ	The perfect perception of vibrations in the subtle body
125	श्रीं	śrīṃ	The perfection of peace in the mind and heart
126	सां	sāṃ	The consciousness of perfect knowledge
127	ह्रीं	hrīṃ	All of Maya: that which can be perceived in the gross body, the subtle body, known through intuition and beyond
128	ऐं	aiṃ	The ultimate wisdom
129	स्क्लीं	sklīṃ	The knowledge of the cause of manifested existence merging into the causal body in perfection

षष्ठोऽध्यायः

ṣaṣṭho-dhyāyaḥ

Chapter Six

1	श्रौं	śrauṃ	The perfection of divine peace in the mind
2	ओं	oṃ	The divine energy of the subtle sound of existence
3	त्रूं	trūṃ	The protection of the perfection of tat twam asi in the mind
4	ह्रौं	hrauṃ	The perfect manifestation of the supreme divinity in the gross and subtle bodies
5	क्रौं	krauṃ	The perfect illumination of the divine cause in the subtle body
6	ह्रीं	hrīṃ	All of Maya: that which can be perceived in the gross body, the subtle body, known through intuition and beyond
7	त्रीं	trīṃ	The manifestation of the perfection of tat twam asi in the mind and heart
8	क्लीं	klīṃ	The cause of manifested existence merging into the causal body in perfection
9	प्रीं	prīṃ	The purity of the mind merging into the causal body in perfection
10	ह्रीं	hrīṃ	All of Maya: that which can be perceived in the gross body, the subtle body, known through intuition and beyond
11	ह्रौं	hrauṃ	The perfect manifestation of the supreme divinity in the gross and subtle bodies
12	श्रौं	śrauṃ	The perfection of divine peace in the mind
13	ऐं	aiṃ	The ultimate wisdom
14	ओं	oṃ	The divine energy of the subtle sound of existence
15	श्रीं	śrīṃ	The perfection of peace in the mind and heart
16	क्रां	krāṃ	The perfect consciousness of the primary cause of existence in the subtle body
17	हूं	hūṃ	The protection of the cutting of the ego
18	छ्रां	chrāṃ	The perfect appearance of consciousness in the subtle body
19	क्ष्म्क्ल्रीं	kṣmklrīṃ	The cause of the perfect measurement from beginning to end
20	ल्लूं	llūṃ	The protection of perfection in the gross body of manifested existence

21	सौं	sauṃ	The perfection of divine knowledge
22	ह्लौं	hlauṃ	The divine perfection that permeates the gross body of manifested existence
23	क्रूं	krūṃ	The protection of the cause of perfection in the subtle body
24	सौं	sauṃ	The perfection of divine knowledge

सप्तमोऽध्यायः

saptamo-dhyāyaḥ

Chapter Seven

1	श्रौं	śrauṃ	The perfection of divine peace in the mind
2	कूं	kūṃ	The cause of perfect protection
3	ह्लीं	hlīṃ	The manifestation of perfection in the gross and causal bodies
4	ह्रं	hraṃ	The perfect manifestation in the gross and subtle bodies
5	मूं	mūṃ	The protection of the measurement of perfection
6	त्रौं	trauṃ	The divinity of the perfection of tat twam asi in the mind
7	ह्रौं	hrauṃ	The perfect manifestation of the supreme divinity in the gross and subtle bodies
8	ओं	oṃ	The divine energy of the subtle sound of existence
9	ह्सूं	hsūṃ	The protection of perfect knowledge in the gross body
10	क्लूं	klūṃ	The cause of the protection of perfection in manifested existence
11	क्रें	kreṃ	The cause of perfect vibrations in the subtle body
12	नें	neṃ	The perfect manifestation of the vibrations of consciousness
13	लूं	lūṃ	The protection of perfection in manifested existence
14	ह्स्लीं	hslīṃ	The perfection of knowledge from manifested existence to the causal body
15	प्लूं	plūṃ	The protection of the perfect purity in manifested existence
16	शां	śāṃ	The consciousness of perfect peace
17	स्लूं	slūṃ	The protection of the perfect knowledge in manifestation
18	प्लीं	plīṃ	The perfect purity in the causal body of manifested existence
19	प्रें	preṃ	The perfect pure vibrations in the mind
20	अं	aṃ	The commencement of creation

21	औं	auṃ	The perfect divinity of all the threes
22	म्ल्रीं	mlrīṃ	The perfect measurement of the subtle and causal bodies of manifested existence
23	श्रां	śrāṃ	The consciousness of perfect peace in the mind
24	सौं	sauṃ	The perfection of divine knowledge
25	श्रौं	śrauṃ	The perfection of divine peace in the mind
26	प्रीं	prīṃ	The purity of the mind merging into the causal body in perfection
27	ह्स्व्रीं	hsvrīṃ	The knowledge of the perfect vibrations which fill the gross, subtle body and causal body

अष्टमोऽध्यायः

aṣṭamo-dhyāyaḥ

Chapter Eight

1	श्रौं	śrauṃ	The perfection of divine peace in the mind
2	म्ह्ल्रीं	mhlrīṃ	The perfect measurement of the gross, subtle, and causal bodies of manifested existence
3	प्रूं	prūṃ	The protection of perfect purity in the mind
4	ऐं	aiṃ	The ultimate wisdom
5	क्रों	kroṃ	The perfection of the subtle sound of the primary cause of existence in the subtle body
6	ईं	īṃ	The cause of perfection
7	ऐं	aiṃ	The ultimate wisdom
8	ल्रीं	lrīṃ	The manifestation of perfection in the subtle and causal bodies
9	फ्रौं	phrauṃ	The perfect divinity of the fruit of karma in the mind
10	म्लूं	mlūṃ	The protection of the perfect measurement of manifested existence
11	नों	noṃ	The consciousness of the subtle sound of manifest existence
12	हूं	hūṃ	The protection of the cutting of the ego
13	फ्रौं	phrauṃ	The perfect divinity of the fruit of karma in the mind
14	ग्लौं	glauṃ	The divine manifestation of the supreme lord of wisdom who removes all obstacles
15	स्मौं	smauṃ	The knowledge of the divine measurement of perfection
16	सौं	sauṃ	The perfection of divine knowledge
17	श्रीं	śrīṃ	The perfection of peace in the mind and heart
18	स्हौं	shauṃ	The perfect divine knowledge that pervades the gross body of existence
19	ख्सें	khseṃ	The perfect vibrations in the sword of knowledge
20	क्ष्म्लीं	kṣmlīṃ	The measurement of perfection of manifested existence to its culmination in the causal body

21	ह्रां	hrāṃ	The perfect consciousness in the gross and subtle bodies
22	वीं	vīṃ	The perfection of vibrations in the causal body
23	लूं	lūṃ	The protection of perfection in manifested existence
24	ल्सीं	lsīṃ	The perfect knowledge of manifested existence in the causal body
25	ब्लीं	blīṃ	The perfection of strength in the causal body of manifested existence
26	त्स्रों	tsroṃ	The perfect subtle of the knowledge of tat twam asi in the mind
27	व्रूं	vrūṃ	The protection of perfect vibrations in the mind
28	श्ल्कीं	ślkīṃ	The peace which causes perfection in the causal body of manifested existence
29	श्रूं	śrūṃ	The protection of perfect peace in the mind
30	ह्रीं	hrīṃ	All of Maya: that which can be perceived in the gross body, the subtle body, known through intuition and beyond
31	शीं	śīṃ	The perfection of peace in the causal body
32	क्लीं	klīṃ	The cause of manifested existence merging into the causal body in perfection
33	क्लौं	klauṃ	The cause of manifested existence merging into divine perfection
34	तीं	tīṃ	The perfection of tat twam asi in the causal body
35	ह्रूं	hrūṃ	The protection of perfection in the gross and subtle bodies
36	क्लूं	klūṃ	The cause of the protection of perfection in manifested existence
37	तां	tāṃ	The perfect consciousness of tat twam asi
38	म्लूं	mlūṃ	The protection of the perfect measurement of manifested existence
39	हं	haṃ	The manifestation of divinity in perceivable form
40	स्लूं	slūṃ	The protection of the perfect knowledge in manifestation
41	औं	auṃ	The perfect divinity of all the threes
42	ल्हों	lhoṃ	The subtle sound of perfection that pervades the gross body of manifested existence
43	श्ल्रीं	ślrīṃ	The perfect peace that pervades the subtle and causal bodies of manifested existence

44	यां	yāṃ	The consciousness of perfect control
45	थ्लीं	thlīṃ	The protection of the perfect prayer in the gross and causal bodies
46	ल्हों	lhoṃ	The subtle sound of perfection that pervades the gross body of manifested existence
47	ग्लौं	glauṃ	The divine manifestation of the supreme lord of wisdom who removes all obstacles
48	ह्रौं	hrauṃ	The perfect manifestation of the supreme divinity in the gross and subtle bodies
49	प्रां	prāṃ	The consciousness of perfect purity in the mind
50	क्रीं	krīṃ	The cause of the subtle body merging into the causal body in perfection
51	क्लीं	klīṃ	The cause of manifested existence merging into the causal body in perfection
52	न्स्लुं	nsluṃ	The consciousness of perfect knowledge of the circumstances of manifested existence
53	हीं	hīṃ	The perfection in the gross and causal bodies
54	ह्लौं	hlauṃ	The divine perfection that permeates the gross body of manifested existence
55	ह्रैं	hraiṃ	The perfection of wisdom in the gross and subtle bodies
56	भ्रं	bhraṃ	The perfect attitude of the mind
57	सौं	sauṃ	The perfection of divine knowledge
58	श्रीं	śrīṃ	The perfection of peace in the mind and heart
59	प्सूं	psūṃ	The protection of the perfect purity of knowledge
60	द्रौं	drauṃ	The perfect perception of the divine mind
61	स्स्रां	ssrāṃ	The consciousness of great knowledge in the perfect mind
62	ह्स्लीं	hslīṃ	The perfection of knowledge from manifested existence to the causal body
63	स्ल्ल्रीं	sllrīṃ	The perfection of knowledge that fills the gross body of manifested existence and the mind

नवमोऽध्यायः

navamo-dhyāyaḥ

Chapter Nine

1	रौं	rauṃ	The divinity manifest in perfection in the subtle body
2	क्लीं	klīṃ	The cause of manifested existence merging into the causal body in perfection
3	म्लौं	mlauṃ	The perfect measurement of divinity in manifested existence
4	श्रौं	śrauṃ	The perfection of divine peace in the mind
5	ग्लीं	glīṃ	The manifestation of the supreme lord of wisdom who removes all obstacles in the causal body
6	ह्रौं	hrauṃ	The perfect manifestation of the supreme divinity in the gross and subtle bodies
7	ह्सौं	hsauṃ	The manifestation of divine knowledge in the gross body
8	ईं	īṃ	The cause of perfection
9	व्रूं	vrūṃ	The protection of perfect vibrations in the mind
10	श्रां	śrāṃ	The consciousness of perfect peace in the mind
11	लूं	lūṃ	The protection of perfection in manifested existence
12	आं	āṃ	The perfect consciousness
13	श्रीं	śrīṃ	The perfection of peace in the mind and heart
14	क्रौं	krauṃ	The perfect illumination of the divine cause in the subtle body
15	प्रूं	prūṃ	The protection of perfect purity in the mind
16	क्लीं	klīṃ	The cause of manifested existence merging into the causal body in perfection
17	भ्रूं	bhrūṃ	The protection of the perfect attitudes of the mind
18	ह्रौं	hrauṃ	The perfect manifestation of the supreme divinity in the gross and subtle bodies
19	क्रीं	krīṃ	The cause of the subtle body merging into the causal body in perfection
20	म्लीं	mlīṃ	The measurement of perfection from manifested existence to the causal body

21	ग्लौं	glauṃ	The divine manifestation of the supreme lord of wisdom who removes all obstacles
22	ह्सूं	hsūṃ	The protection of perfect knowledge in the gross body
23	ल्पीं	lpīṃ	The perfect purity in the causal body of manifested existence
24	ह्रौं	hrauṃ	The perfect manifestation of the supreme divinity in the gross and subtle bodies
25	ह्स्रां	hsrāṃ	The consciousness of perfect knowledge in the gross and subtle bodies
26	स्हौं	shauṃ	The perfect divine knowledge that pervades the gross body of existence
27	ल्लूं	llūṃ	The protection of perfection in the gross body of manifested existence
28	क्स्लीं	kslīṃ	The cause of perfect knowledge in the gross body and causal bodies
29	श्रीं	śrīṃ	The perfection of peace in the mind and heart
30	स्तूं	stūṃ	The protection of the perfect knowledge of tat twam asi
31	च्रें	creṃ	The consciousness of perfect vibrations in the mind
32	वीं	vīṃ	The perfection of vibrations in the causal body
33	क्ष्लूं	kṣlūṃ	The protection of the perfect completion of manifested existence
34	श्लूं	ślūṃ	The protection of perfect peace in manifested existence
35	क्रूं	krūṃ	The protection of the cause of perfection in the subtle body
36	क्रां	krāṃ	The perfect consciousness of the primary cause of existence in the subtle body
37	ह्रौं	hrauṃ	The perfect manifestation of the supreme divinity in the gross and subtle bodies
38	क्रां	krāṃ	The perfect consciousness of the primary cause of existence in the subtle body
39	स्क्ष्लीं	skṣlīṃ	The culmination of perfect knowledge from manifested existence to the causal body
40	सूं	sūṃ	The protection of the perfect knowledge
41	फ्रूं	phrūṃ	The protection of the perfect fruit of karma in the mind

दशमोऽध्यायः

daśamo-dhyāyaḥ

Chapter Ten

1	श्रौं	śrauṃ	The perfection of divine peace in the mind
2	ह्रीं	hrīṃ	All of Maya: that which can be perceived in the gross body, the subtle body, known through intuition and beyond
3	ब्लूं	blūṃ	The protection of perfect strength in manifested existence
4	ह्रीं	hrīṃ	All of Maya: that which can be perceived in the gross body, the subtle body, known through intuition and beyond
5	म्लूं	mlūṃ	The protection of the perfect measurement of manifested existence
6	श्रौं	śrauṃ	The perfection of divine peace in the mind
7	ह्रीं	hrīṃ	All of Maya: that which can be perceived in the gross body, the subtle body, known through intuition and beyond
8	ग्लीं	glīṃ	The manifestation of the supreme lord of wisdom who removes all obstacles in the causal body
9	श्रौं	śrauṃ	The perfection of divine peace in the mind
10	ध्रूं	dhrūṃ	The protection of the mind in perfect meditation
11	हुं	huṃ	The perfection of the circumstances of the gross body
12	द्रौं	drauṃ	The perfect perception of the divine mind
13	श्रीं	śrīṃ	The perfection of peace in the mind and heart
14	त्रूं	trūṃ	The protection of the perfection of tat twam asi in the mind
15	व्रूं	vrūṃ	The protection of perfect vibrations in the mind
16	फ्रें	phreṃ	The perfect wisdom of the fruit of karma in the mind
17	ह्रां	hrāṃ	The perfect consciousness in the gross and subtle bodies
18	जुं	juṃ	The perfection of the birth of all circumstances
19	स्त्रौं	strauṃ	The perfection of the divine knowledge of tat twam asi in the mind

20	स्लूं	slūṃ	The protection of the perfect knowledge in manifestation
21	प्रें	preṃ	The perfect pure vibrations in the mind
22	ह्स्वां	hsvāṃ	The perfect consciousness of the vibrations of knowledge in the gross body
23	प्रीं	prīṃ	The purity of the mind merging into the causal body in perfection
24	फ्रां	phrāṃ	The consciousness of the fruit of perfect karma in the mind
25	क्रीं	krīṃ	The cause of the subtle body merging into the causal body in perfection
26	श्रीं	śrīṃ	The perfection of peace in the mind and heart
27	क्रां	krāṃ	The perfect consciousness of the primary cause of existence in the subtle body
28	सः	saḥ	The perfect knowledge of name and form
29	क्लीं	klīṃ	The cause of manifested existence merging into the causal body in perfection
30	व्रें	vreṃ	The perfect vibrations of wisdom in the mind
31	ईं	īṃ	The cause of perfection
32	ज्स्ह्ल्रीं	jshlrīṃ	The perfection of the knowledge of all beings born in the gross, subtle and causal bodies of manifested existence

एकादशोऽध्यायः

ekādaśo-dhyāyaḥ

Chapter Eleven

1	श्रौं	śrauṃ	The perfection of divine peace in the mind
2	क्रूं	krūṃ	The protection of the cause of perfection in the subtle body
3	श्रीं	śrīṃ	The perfection of peace in the mind and heart
4	ल्लीं	llīṃ	The perfect manifestation in the gross and causal bodies
5	प्रें	preṃ	The perfect pure vibrations in the mind
6	सौं	sauṃ	The perfection of divine knowledge
7	स्हौं	shauṃ	The perfect divine knowledge that pervades the gross body of existence
8	श्रूं	śrūṃ	The protection of perfect peace in the mind
9	क्लीं	klīṃ	The cause of manifested existence merging into the causal body in perfection
10	स्क्लीं	sklīṃ	The knowledge of the cause of manifested existence merging into the causal body in perfection
11	प्रीं	prīṃ	The purity of the mind merging into the causal body in perfection
12	ग्लौं	glauṃ	The divine manifestation of the supreme lord of wisdom who removes all obstacles
13	ह्स्ह्रीं	hshrīṃ	The gross form of knowledge that fills the gross, subtle and causal bodies
14	स्तौं	stauṃ	The perfect divine knowledge of tat twam asi
15	लीं	līṃ	The perfect manifestation in the causal body
16	म्लीं	mlīṃ	The measurement of perfection from manifested existence to the causal body
17	स्तूं	stūṃ	The protection of the perfect knowledge of tat twam asi
18	ज्स्ह्रीं	jshnīṃ	The perfect knowledge of all beings born in the gross and causal bodies
19	फ्रूं	phrūṃ	The protection of the perfect fruit of karma in the mind
20	क्रूं	krūṃ	The protection of the cause of perfection in the subtle body

21	ह्रीं	hrīṃ	All of Maya: that which can be perceived in the gross body, the subtle body, known through intuition and beyond
22	ऌूं	llūṃ	The protection of perfection in the gross body of manifested existence
23	क्ष्म्रीं	kṣmrīṃ	The measurement of the culmination of perfection in the mind and heart
24	श्रूं	śrūṃ	The protection of perfect peace in the mind
25	इं	iṃ	The perfection of the full and complete meaning
26	जुं	juṃ	The perfection of the birth of all circumstances
27	त्रैं	traiṃ	The perfect wisdom of tat twam asi in the mind
28	द्रूं	drūṃ	The protection of perfect perception in the mind
29	ह्रौं	hrauṃ	The perfect manifestation of the supreme divinity in the gross and subtle bodies
30	क्लीं	klīṃ	The cause of manifested existence merging into the causal body in perfection
31	सूं	sūṃ	The protection of the perfect knowledge
32	हौं	hauṃ	The perfect divinity in the gross body
33	श्वं	śvraṃ	The perfection of peaceful vibrations in the mind
34	व्रूं	vrūṃ	The protection of perfect vibrations in the mind
35	फां	phāṃ	The consciousness of the fruit of perfect karma
36	ह्रीं	hrīṃ	All of Maya: that which can be perceived in the gross body, the subtle body, known through intuition and beyond
37	लं	laṃ	The perfection of manifested existence
38	ह्सौं	hsauṃ	The manifestation of divine knowledge in the gross body
39	सें	seṃ	The knowledge of the perfect vibrations
40	ह्रीं	hrīṃ	All of Maya: that which can be perceived in the gross body, the subtle body, known through intuition and beyond
41	ह्रौं	hrauṃ	The perfect manifestation of the supreme divinity in the gross and subtle bodies
42	विं	viṃ	The vibrations of perfect knowledge

43	प्लीं	plīṃ	The perfect purity in the causal body of manifested existence
44	क्ष्म्क्लीं	kṣmklīṃ	The measurement of the cause of perfection from manifested existence to the causal body from beginning to end
45	त्स्रां	tsrāṃ	The perfect consciousness of the knowledge of tat twam asi in the mind
46	प्रं	praṃ	The perfect purity of the mind
47	म्लीं	mlīṃ	The measurement of perfection from manifested existence to the causal body
48	स्रूं	srūṃ	The protection of perfect knowledge in the mind
49	क्ष्मां	kṣmāṃ	The culmination of the measurement of perfect consciousness
50	स्तूं	stūṃ	The protection of the perfect knowledge of tat twam asi
51	स्ह्रीं	shrīṃ	The knowledge that fills the gross, subtle and causal bodies
52	थ्प्रीं	thprīṃ	The perfect purity of prayer in the subtle and causal bodies
53	क्रौं	krauṃ	The perfect illumination of the divine cause in the subtle body
54	श्रां	śrāṃ	The consciousness of perfect peace in the mind
55	म्लीं	mlīṃ	The measurement of perfection from manifested existence to the causal body

द्वादशोऽध्यायः

dvādaśo-dhyāyaḥ

Chapter Twelve

1	ह्रीं	hrīṃ	All of Maya: that which can be perceived in the gross body, the subtle body, known through intuition and beyond
2	ओं	oṃ	The divine energy of the subtle sound of existence
3	श्रीं	śrīṃ	The perfection of peace in the mind and heart
4	ईं	īṃ	The cause of perfection
5	क्लीं	klīṃ	The cause of manifested existence merging into the causal body in perfection
6	क्रूं	krūṃ	The protection of the cause of perfection in the subtle body
7	श्रूं	śrūṃ	The protection of perfect peace in the mind
8	प्रां	prāṃ	The consciousness of perfect purity in the mind
9	क्रूं	krūṃ	The protection of the cause of perfection in the subtle body
10	दिं	diṃ	The perfect perception of the full and complete meaning
11	फ्रें	phreṃ	The perfect wisdom of the fruit of karma in the mind
12	हं	haṃ	The manifestation of divinity in perceivable form
13	सः	saḥ	The perfect knowledge of name and form
14	चें	ceṃ	The vibrations of perfect consciousness
15	सूं	sūṃ	The protection of the perfect knowledge
16	प्रीं	prīṃ	The purity of the mind merging into the causal body in perfection
17	व्लूं	vlūṃ	The protection of the perfect vibrations of manifested existence
18	आं	āṃ	The perfect consciousness
19	औं	auṃ	The perfect divinity of all the threes
20	ह्रीं	hrīṃ	All of Maya: that which can be perceived in the gross body, the subtle body, known through intuition and beyond

21	क्रीं	krīṃ	The cause of the subtle body merging into the causal body in perfection
22	द्रां	drāṃ	The perfect perception of consciousness in the mind
23	श्रीं	śrīṃ	The perfection of peace in the mind and heart
24	स्लीं	slīṃ	The knowledge of the perfect union of manifested existence with the causal body
25	क्लीं	klīṃ	The cause of manifested existence merging into the causal body in perfection
26	स्लूं	slūṃ	The protection of the perfect knowledge in manifestation
27	ह्रीं	hrīṃ	All of Maya: that which can be perceived in the gross body, the subtle body, known through intuition and beyond
28	व्लीं	vlīṃ	The perfection of the vibrations of manifested existence in the causal body
29	त्रों	troṃ	The manifestation of the perfection of tat twam asi in the subtle body
30	ओं	oṃ	The divine energy of the subtle sound of existence
31	श्रौं	śrauṃ	The perfection of divine peace in the mind
32	ऐं	aiṃ	The ultimate wisdom
33	प्रें	preṃ	The perfect pure vibrations in the mind
34	द्रूं	drūṃ	The protection of perfect perception in the mind
35	क्लूं	klūṃ	The cause of the protection of perfection in manifested existence
36	औं	auṃ	The perfect divinity of all the threes
37	सूं	sūṃ	The protection of the perfect knowledge
38	चें	ceṃ	The vibrations of perfect consciousness
39	ह्रूं	hrūṃ	The protection of perfection in the gross and subtle bodies
40	प्लीं	plīṃ	The perfect purity in the causal body of manifested existence
41	क्षां	kṣāṃ	The culmination of perfect consciousness

त्रयोदशोऽध्यायः

trayodaśo-dhyāyaḥ

Chapter Thirteen

1	श्रौं	śrauṃ	The perfection of divine peace in the mind
2	व्रीं	vrīṃ	The perfection of vibrations in the mind and heart
3	ओं	oṃ	The divine energy of the subtle sound of existence
4	औं	auṃ	The perfect divinity of all the threes
5	ह्रां	hrāṃ	The perfect consciousness in the gross and subtle bodies
6	श्रीं	śrīṃ	The perfection of peace in the mind and heart
7	श्रां	śrāṃ	The consciousness of perfect peace in the mind
8	ओं	oṃ	The divine energy of the subtle sound of existence
9	प्लीं	plīṃ	The perfect purity in the causal body of manifested existence
10	सौं	sauṃ	The perfection of divine knowledge
11	ह्रीं	hrīṃ	All of Maya: that which can be perceived in the gross body, the subtle body, known through intuition and beyond
12	क्रीं	krīṃ	The cause of the subtle body merging into the causal body in perfection
13	ल्लूं	llūṃ	The protection of perfection in the gross body of manifested existence
14	क्लीं	klīṃ	The cause of manifested existence merging into the causal body in perfection
15	ह्रीं	hrīṃ	All of Maya: that which can be perceived in the gross body, the subtle body, known through intuition and beyond
16	प्लीं	plīṃ	The perfect purity in the causal body of manifested existence
17	श्रीं	śrīṃ	The perfection of peace in the mind and heart
18	ल्लीं	llīṃ	The perfect manifestation in the gross and causal bodies
19	श्रूं	śrūṃ	The protection of perfect peace in the mind
20	ह्रीं	hrīṃ	All of Maya: that which can be perceived in the gross body, the subtle body, known through intuition and beyond

21	त्रूं	trūṃ	The protection of the perfection of tat twam asi in the mind
22	ह्रीं	hrīṃ	All of Maya: that which can be perceived in the gross body, the subtle body, known through intuition and beyond
23	ह्रां	hrāṃ	The perfect consciousness in the gross and subtle bodies
24	प्रीं	prīṃ	The purity of the mind merging into the causal body in perfection
25	ॐ	oṃ	The infinite beyond conception
26	सूं	sūṃ	The protection of the perfect knowledge
27	ह्लौं	hlauṃ	The divine perfection that permeates the gross body of manifested existence
28	षौं	ṣauṃ	The divine peace which resides in bliss
29	आं ल्क्रीं	āṃ lkrīṃ	The perfect consciousness of the manifested cause of perfection in the mind and heart
30	ओं	oṃ	The divine energy of the subtle sound of existence

इति त्रयोदशोऽध्यायः

iti trayodaśo-dhyāyaḥ

Here ends Chapter Thirteen

तन्त्ररूपन्देवी सूक्तम्

tantrarūpandevī sūktam

Tantrik Form of the Praise of the Goddess

1	ह्सौं	hsoṃ	The manifestation of perfect divine knowledge in the gross body
2	ह्रीं	hrīṃ	All of Maya: that which can be perceived in the gross body, the subtle body, known through intuition and beyond
3	श्रीं	śrīṃ	The perfection of peace in the mind and heart
4	हूं	hūṃ	The protection of the cutting of the ego
5	क्लीं	klīṃ	The cause of manifested existence merging into the causal body in perfection
6	रौं	rauṃ	The divinity manifest in perfection in the subtle body
7	स्त्रीं	strīṃ	The perfection of the knowledge of tat twam asi in the subtle and causal bodies
8	म्लीं	mlīṃ	The measurement of perfection from manifested existence to the causal body
9	प्लूं	plūṃ	The protection of the perfect purity in manifested existence
10	स्हौं	shauṃ	The perfect divine knowledge that pervades the gross body of existence
11	स्त्रीं	strīṃ	The perfection of the knowledge of tat twam asi in the subtle and causal bodies
12	ग्लूं	glūṃ	The protection of the manifestation of the supreme lord of wisdom who removes all obstacles
13	व्रीं	vrīṃ	The perfection of vibrations in the mind and heart
14	सौं	sauṃ	The perfection of divine knowledge
15	लूं	lūṃ	The protection of perfection in manifested existence
16	ल्लूं	llūṃ	The protection of perfection in the gross body of manifested existence
17	द्रां	drāṃ	The perfect perception of consciousness in the mind
18	क्सां	ksāṃ	The cause of the perfection of the consciousness of divine knowledge
19	क्ष्म्रीं	kṣmrīṃ	The measurement of the culmination of perfection in the mind and heart
20	ग्लौं	glauṃ	The divine manifestation of the supreme lord of wisdom who removes all obstacles

21	स्कं	skaṃ	The knowledge of the perfect beginning
22	त्रूं	trūṃ	The protection of the perfection of tat twam asi in the mind
23	स्क्लूं	sklūṃ	The knowledge which causes the protection of perfection in manifested existence
24	क्रौं	krauṃ	The perfect illumination of the divine cause in the subtle body
25	श्रीं	śrīṃ	The perfection of peace in the mind and heart
26	म्लूं	mlūṃ	The protection of the perfect measurement of manifested existence
27	क्लूं	klūṃ	The cause of the protection of perfection in manifested existence
28	शां	śāṃ	The consciousness of perfect peace
29	ल्हीं	lhīṃ	The manifestation of perfection in the gross and causal bodies
30	स्रूं	srūṃ	The protection of perfect knowledge in the mind
31	ल्लीं	llīṃ	The perfect manifestation in the gross and causal bodies
32	लीं	līṃ	The perfect manifestation in the causal body
33	सं	saṃ	The manifestation of perfect knowledge
34	लूं	lūṃ	The protection of perfection in manifested existence
35	ह्सूं	hsūṃ	The protection of perfect knowledge in the gross body
36	श्रूं	śrūṃ	The protection of perfect peace in the mind
37	जूं	jūṃ	The protection of perfection in all beings born
38	ह्स्ल्रीं	hslrīṃ	The perfect knowledge which manifests in the gross, subtle and causal bodies of manifested existence
39	स्कीं	skīṃ	The cause of perfect knowledge in the causal body
40	क्लां	klāṃ	The cause of the perfect consciousness in manifested existence
41	श्रूं	śrūṃ	The protection of perfect peace in the mind
42	हं	haṃ	The manifestation of divinity in perceivable form
43	ह्लीं	hlīṃ	The manifestation of perfection in the gross and causal bodies

44	क्स्रूं	ksrūṃ	The cause of protection of perfect knowledge in the mind
45	द्रौं	drauṃ	The perfect perception of the divine mind
46	क्लूं	klūṃ	The cause of the protection of perfection in manifested existence
47	गां	gāṃ	The perfect consciousness of the supreme lord of wisdom who removes all obstacles
48	सं	saṃ	The manifestation of perfect knowledge
49	ल्स्रां	lsrāṃ	The perfect knowledge which makes consciousness manifest in the mind
50	फ्रीं	phrīṃ	The perfection of the fruit of karma in the mind and heart
51	स्लां	slāṃ	The knowledge of the perfect consciousness in manifested existence
52	ल्लूं	llūṃ	The protection of perfection in the gross body of manifested existence
53	फ्रें	phreṃ	The perfect wisdom of the fruit of karma in the mind
54	ओं	oṃ	The divine energy of the subtle sound of existence
55	स्म्लीं	smlīṃ	The perfect knowledge of the measurement from manifested existence to the causal body
56	ह्रां	hrāṃ	The perfect consciousness in the gross and subtle bodies
57	ॐ	oṃ	The infinite beyond conception
58	ह्लूं	hlūṃ	The protection of the manifestation of perfection in the gross body
59	हूं	hūṃ	The protection of the cutting of the ego
60	नं	naṃ	The manifestation of the perfect embodiment of consciousness
61	स्रां	srāṃ	The knowledge of perfect consciousness in the mind
62	वं	vaṃ	The perfection of all vibrations
63	मं	maṃ	The measurement of perfection
64	म्क्लीं	mklīṃ	The cause of the measurement of perfection in the gross and subtle bodies
65	शां	śāṃ	The consciousness of perfect peace
66	लं	laṃ	The perfection of manifested existence

67	भौं	bhauṃ	The perfect divine attitude
68	ल्लूं	llūṃ	The protection of perfection in the gross body of manifested existence
69	हौं	hauṃ	The perfect divinity in the gross body
70	ईं	īṃ	The cause of perfection
71	चें	ceṃ	The vibrations of perfect consciousness
72	ल्क्रीं	lkrīṃ	The manifested cause of perfection in the mind and the heart
73	ह्ल्रीं	hlrīṃ	The manifestation of perfection in the gross, subtle and causal bodies
74	क्ष्म्ल्रीं	kṣmlrīṃ	The culmination of the measurement of the manifestation of perfection in the gross, subtle and causal bodies
75	पूं	pūṃ	The protection of perfect purity
76	श्रौं	śrauṃ	The perfection of divine peace in the mind
77	ह्रौं	hrauṃ	The perfect manifestation of the supreme divinity in the gross and subtle bodies
78	भ्रूं	bhrūṃ	The protection of the perfect attitudes of the mind
79	क्स्त्रीं	kstrīṃ	The cause of the knowledge of tat twam asi in the mind and heart
80	आं	āṃ	The perfect consciousness
81	क्रूं	krūṃ	The protection of the cause of perfection in the subtle body
82	त्रूं	trūṃ	The protection of the perfection of tat twam asi in the mind

Bīja Mantras – Alphabetical Listing

ऐं	aiṃ	The ultimate wisdom
अं	aṃ	The commencement of creation
आं	āṃ	The perfect consciousness
आं ल्क्रीं	āṃ lkrīṃ	The perfect consciousness of the manifested cause of perfection in the mind and heart
औं	auṃ	The perfect divinity of all the threes
भौं	bhauṃ	The perfect divine attitude
भ्रं	bhraṃ	The perfect attitude of the mind
भ्रूं	bhrūṃ	The protection of the perfect attitudes of the mind
भूं	bhūṃ	The protection of the perfect attitude
ब्लं	blaṃ	The perfection of strength in manifested existence
ब्लीं	blīṃ	The perfection of strength in the causal body of manifested existence
ब्लूं	blūṃ	The protection of perfect strength in manifested existence
ब्रीं	brīṃ	The cause of perfect strength in the mind
बूं	būṃ	The protection of perfect strength
चां	cāṃ	The perfect manifestation of consciousness
च्चें	cceṃ	The perfection of union between consciousness and wisdom
च्छ्रूं	cchrūṃ	The protection of the perfect appearance of consciousness in the subtle body
चें	ceṃ	The vibrations of perfect consciousness
छां	chāṃ	The consciousness of the reflection of perfection
छ्रां	chrāṃ	The perfect appearance of consciousness in the subtle body
छ्रीं	chrīṃ	The perfect reflection in the mind and heart

छ्रक्लीं	chrklīṃ	The cause of the perfect appearance of the gross, subtle and causal bodies
च्रें	creṃ	The consciousness of perfect vibrations in the mind
दं	daṃ	The perception of perfection
डां	ḍāṃ	The perfect consciousness of worship with excessive devotion
दें	deṃ	The perception of the vibrations of perfection
डें	ḍeṃ	The perfect vibrations of worship with excessive devotion
ध्रूं	dhrūṃ	The protection of the mind in perfect meditation
धूं	dhūṃ	The protection of the perfect meditation
दिं	diṃ	The perfect perception of the full and complete meaning
दीं	dīṃ	The perfect perception in the causal body
द्लूं	dlūṃ	The protection of the perception of the perfect manifested existence
द्रां	drāṃ	The perfect perception of consciousness in the mind
द्रौं	drauṃ	The perfect perception of the divine mind
द्रें	dreṃ	The perfect perception of vibrations in the subtle body
द्रों	droṃ	The perfect perception with full and complete consciousness in God
द्रूं	drūṃ	The protection of perfect perception in the mind
दुं	duṃ	The perfect perception of all circumstances
डुं	ḍuṃ	The circumstance of perfect devotion to the Divine Mother
डूं	ḍūṃ	The protection of the perfect love for Divine Mother with excessive devotion
गैं	gaiṃ	The perfect wisdom of the supreme lord of wisdom who removes all obstacles
गं	gaṃ	The supreme lord of wisdom who removes all obstacles
गां	gāṃ	The perfect consciousness of the supreme lord of wisdom who removes all obstacles
घ्रें	ghreṃ	The vibrations which remove fear from the mind

गीं	gīṃ	The perfection in the heart of the supreme lord of wisdom who removes all obstacles
ग्लौं	glauṃ	The divine manifestation of the supreme lord of wisdom who removes all obstacles
ग्लीं	glīṃ	The manifestation of the supreme lord of wisdom who removes all obstacles in the causal body
ग्लूं	glūṃ	The protection of the manifestation of the supreme lord of wisdom who removes all obstacles
ग्रीं	grīṃ	The perfect manifestation of the supreme lord of wisdom in the mind and heart
गूं	gūṃ	The perfect protection of the supreme lord of wisdom who removes all obstacles
हं	haṃ	The manifestation of divinity in perceivable form
हौं	hauṃ	The perfect divinity in the gross body
हीं	hīṃ	The perfection in the gross and causal bodies
ह्लौं	hlauṃ	The divine perfection that permeates the gross body of manifested existence
ह्लीं	hlīṃ	The manifestation of perfection in the gross and causal bodies
ह्ल्लौं	hllauṃ	The divine perfection which permeates the gross body of manifested existence
ह्ल्रीं	hlrīṃ	The manifestation of perfection in the gross, subtle and causal bodies
ह्ल्रूं	hlrūṃ	The perfect protection in the gross and subtle bodies of manifested existence
ह्लूं	hlūṃ	The protection of the manifestation of perfection in the gross body
ह्रैं	hraiṃ	The perfection of wisdom in the gross and subtle bodies
ह्रं	hraṃ	The perfect manifestation in the gross and subtle bodies
ह्रां	hrāṃ	The perfect consciousness in the gross and subtle bodies
ह्रौं	hrauṃ	The perfect manifestation of the supreme divinity in the gross and subtle bodies
ह्रीं	hrīṃ	All of Maya: that which can be perceived in the gross body, the subtle body, known through intuition and beyond
ह्रूं	hrūṃ	The protection of perfection in the gross and subtle bodies
ह्सौं	hsauṃ	The manifestation of divine knowledge in the gross body

ह्स्ह्रीं	hshrīṃ	The gross form of knowledge that fills the gross, subtle and causal bodies
ह्स्ली	hslīṃ	The perfection of knowledge from manifested existence to the causal body
ह्स्ल्रीं	hslrīṃ	The perfect knowledge which manifests in the gross, subtle and causal bodies of manifested existence
ह्सों	hsoṃ	The manifestation of perfect divine knowledge in the gross body
ह्स्रां	hsrāṃ	The consciousness of perfect knowledge in the gross and subtle bodies
ह्सूं	hsūṃ	The protection of perfect knowledge in the gross body
ह्स्वां	hsvāṃ	The perfect consciousness of the vibrations of knowledge in the gross body
ह्स्व्रीं	hsvrīṃ	The knowledge of the perfect vibrations which fill the gross, subtle body and causal body
हुं	huṃ	The perfection of the circumstances of the gross body
हूँ	hūm̐	The protection of the cutting of the ego
हूं	hūṃ	The protection of the cutting of the ego
इं	iṃ	The perfection of the full and complete meaning
ईं	īṃ	The cause of perfection
जां	jāṃ	The perfection of consciousness in all beings born
जीं	jīṃ	The perfection of all beings born in the causal body
ज्रां	jrāṃ	The perfect understanding of the minds of all living beings
ज्स्ह्ल्रीं	jshlrīṃ	The perfection of the knowledge of all beings born in the gross, subtle and causal bodies of manifested existence
ज्स्ह्नीं	jshnīṃ	The perfect knowledge of all beings born in the gross and causal bodies
जुं	juṃ	The perfection of the birth of all circumstances
जूं	jūṃ	The protection of perfection in all beings born
ज्यैं	jyaiṃ	The perfect control with wisdom for all beings born
कं	kaṃ	The cause of the perfect beginning

ख्सें	khseṃ	The perfect vibrations in the sword of knowledge
किं	kiṃ	The cause of perfection of the full and complete meaning
क्लं	klaṃ	The cause of perfection in manifested existence
क्लां	klāṃ	The cause of the perfect consciousness in manifested existence
क्लौं	klauṃ	The cause of manifested existence merging into divine perfection
क्लीं	klīṃ	The cause of manifested existence merging into the causal body in perfection
क्लूं	klūṃ	The cause of the protection of perfection in manifested existence
क्रैं	kraiṃ	The cause of perfect wisdom in the mind
क्रं	kraṃ	The cause of the perfection in the subtle body
क्रां	krāṃ	The perfect consciousness of the primary cause of existence in the subtle body
क्रौं	krauṃ	The perfect illumination of the divine cause in the subtle body
क्रें	kreṃ	The cause of perfect vibrations in the subtle body
क्रीं	krīṃ	The cause of the subtle body merging into the causal body in perfection
क्रों	kroṃ	The perfection of the subtle sound of the primary cause of existence in the subtle body
क्रूं	krūṃ	The protection of the cause of perfection in the subtle body
क्सैं	ksaiṃ	The cause of perfect knowledge which yields wisdom
क्सां	ksāṃ	The cause of the perfection of the consciousness of divine knowledge
क्षं	kṣaṃ	The completion of the pilgrimage in perfection
क्षां	kṣāṃ	The culmination of perfect consciousness
क्सीं	ksīṃ	The cause of the perfection of divine knowledge in the causal body
क्स्लीं	kslīṃ	The cause of perfect knowledge in the gross body and causal bodies
क्ष्लूं	kṣlūṃ	The protection of the perfect completion of manifested existence
क्ष्मां	kṣmāṃ	The culmination of the measurement of perfect consciousness

क्ष्म्क्लीं	kṣmklīṃ	The measurement of the cause of perfection from manifested existence to the causal body from beginning to end
क्ष्म्क्लृीं	kṣmklrīṃ	The cause of the perfect measurement from beginning to end
क्ष्म्लीं	kṣmlīṃ	The measurement of perfection of manifested existence to its culmination in the causal body
क्ष्म्लृीं	kṣmlrīṃ	The culmination of the measurement of the manifestation of perfection in the gross, subtle and causal bodies
क्ष्म्रीं	kṣmrīṃ	The measurement of the culmination of perfection in the mind and heart
क्स्रूं	ksrūṃ	The cause of protection of perfect knowledge in the mind
क्स्त्रीं	kstrīṃ	The cause of the knowledge of tat twam asi in the mind and heart
कुं	kuṃ	The cause of the perfect circumstance
कूं	kūṃ	The cause of perfect protection
लं	laṃ	The perfection of manifested existence
लां	lāṃ	The perfect manifestation of consciousness
ल्हीं	lhīṃ	The manifestation of perfection in the gross and causal bodies
ल्हों	lhoṃ	The subtle sound of perfection that pervades the gross body of manifested existence
ल्हूं	lhūṃ	The protection of perfection in the gross body of manifested existence
लीं	līṃ	The perfect manifestation in the causal body
ल्क्रीं	lkrīṃ	The manifested cause of perfection in the mind and the heart
ल्लीं	llīṃ	The perfect manifestation in the gross and causal bodies
ल्लूं	llūṃ	The protection of perfection in the gross body of manifested existence
ल्पीं	lpīṃ	The perfect purity in the causal body of manifested existence
लृीं	lrīṃ	The manifestation of perfection in the subtle and causal bodies
ल्सीं	lsīṃ	The perfect knowledge of manifested existence in the causal body
ल्स्रां	lsrāṃ	The perfect knowledge which makes consciousness manifest in the mind

लूं	lūṃ	The protection of perfection in manifested existence
ल्वां	lvāṃ	The consciousness of perfect vibrations in manifested existence
मं	maṃ	The measurement of perfection
में	meṃ	The measurement of the perfection of vibrations
म्हौं	mhauṃ	The measurement of perfect divinity in the gross body
म्ह्ल्रीं	mhlrīṃ	The perfect measurement of the gross, subtle, and causal bodies of manifested existence
मीं	mīṃ	The perfect measurement of the causal body
म्क्लीं	mklīṃ	The cause of the measurement of perfection in the gross and subtle bodies
म्ल्रीं	mlrīṃ	The perfect measurement of the subtle and causal bodies of manifested existence
म्लौं	mlauṃ	The perfect measurement of divinity in manifested existence
म्लीं	mlīṃ	The measurement of perfection from manifested existence to the causal body
म्लूं	mlūṃ	The protection of the perfect measurement of manifested existence
म्रीं	mrīṃ	The measurement of perfection in the subtle and causal bodies
मुं	muṃ	The measurement of the circumstances of perfection
मूं	mūṃ	The protection of the measurement of perfection
म्व्लीं	mvlīṃ	The measurement of the perfect vibrations from manifested existence to the causal body
नं	naṃ	The manifestation of the perfect embodiment of consciousness
नें	neṃ	The perfect manifestation of the vibrations of consciousness
नों	noṃ	The consciousness of the subtle sound of manifest existence
न्स्लुं	nsluṃ	The consciousness of perfect knowledge of the circumstances of manifested existence
नूं	nūṃ	The protection of perfect consciousness
ङूं	ṅūṃ	The protection of that which causes the end to duality

ॐ	oṃ	The infinite beyond conception
ओं	oṃ	The divine energy of the subtle sound of existence
फां	phāṃ	The consciousness of the fruit of perfect karma
फ्रैं	phraiṃ	The perfection of the fruit of wisdom of karma in the mind
फ्रां	phrāṃ	The consciousness of the fruit of perfect karma in the mind
फ्रौं	phrauṃ	The perfect divinity of the fruit of karma in the mind
फ्रें	phreṃ	The perfect wisdom of the fruit of karma in the mind
फ्रीं	phrīṃ	The perfection of the fruit of karma in the mind and heart
फ्रूं	phrūṃ	The protection of the perfect fruit of karma in the mind
प्लीं	plīṃ	The perfect purity in the causal body of manifested existence
प्लूं	plūṃ	The protection of the perfect purity in manifested existence
प्रं	praṃ	The perfect purity of the mind
प्रां	prāṃ	The consciousness of perfect purity in the mind
प्रें	preṃ	The perfect pure vibrations in the mind
प्रीं	prīṃ	The purity of the mind merging into the causal body in perfection
प्रूं	prūṃ	The protection of perfect purity in the mind
प्सूं	psūṃ	The protection of the perfect purity of knowledge
पूं	pūṃ	The protection of perfect purity
रं	raṃ	The perfection in the subtle body
रौं	rauṃ	The divinity manifest in perfection in the subtle body
ऋं	ṛṃ	The perfect attitude of a seer of divine inspiration
रूं	rūṃ	The protection of the perfect mind
सः	saḥ	The perfect knowledge of name and form

सं	saṃ	The manifestation of perfect knowledge
सां	sāṃ	The consciousness of perfect knowledge
शं	śaṃ	The perfection of peace
शां	śāṃ	The consciousness of perfect peace
सौं	sauṃ	The perfection of divine knowledge
शौं	śauṃ	The perfection of divine peace
षौं	ṣauṃ	The divine peace which resides in bliss
स्भ्रूं	sbhrūṃ	The protection of the knowledge of the perfect attitudes of the mind
सें	seṃ	The knowledge of the perfect vibrations
स्हैं	shaiṃ	The knowledge of the perfection of wisdom in the gross body
स्हौं	shauṃ	The perfect divine knowledge that pervades the gross body of existence
स्ह्रीं	shrīṃ	The knowledge that fills the gross, subtle and causal bodies
स्हुं	shuṃ	The knowledge that brings perfection to the circumstances of the gross body
सीं	sīṃ	The perfection of divine knowledge in the causal body
शीं	śīṃ	The perfection of peace in the causal body
स्कं	skaṃ	The knowledge of the perfect beginning
स्कीं	skīṃ	The cause of perfect knowledge in the causal body
स्क्लीं	sklīṃ	The knowledge of the cause of manifested existence merging into the causal body in perfection
स्क्लूं	sklūṃ	The knowledge which causes the protection of perfection in manifested existence
स्क्रीं	skrīṃ	The knowledge which causes perfection in the mind and heart
स्क्ष्लीं	skṣlīṃ	The culmination of perfect knowledge from manifested existence to the causal body
स्लां	slāṃ	The knowledge of the perfect consciousness in manifested existence

स्लीं	slīṃ	The knowledge of the perfect union of manifested existence with the causal body
श्ल्कीं	ślkīṃ	The peace which causes perfection in the causal body of manifested existence
स्ल्ल्रीं	sllrīṃ	The perfection of knowledge that fills the gross body of manifested existence and the mind
श्ल्रीं	ślrīṃ	The perfect peace that pervades the subtle and causal bodies of manifested existence
श्लूं	ślūṃ	The protection of perfect peace in manifested existence
स्मौं	smauṃ	The knowledge of the divine measurement of perfection
स्म्लीं	smlīṃ	The perfect knowledge of the measurement from manifested existence to the causal body
स्मूं	smūṃ	The protection of the measurement of perfect knowledge
सों	soṃ	The manifestation of perfect divine knowledge
श्रां	śrāṃ	The consciousness of perfect peace in the mind
श्रौं	śrauṃ	The perfection of divine peace in the mind
स्रीं	srīṃ	The perfect knowledge in the mind and heart
श्रीं	śrīṃ	The perfection of peace in the mind and heart
श्श्रीं	śrśrīṃ	The perfection of more peace in your mind and heart
स्रूं	srūṃ	The protection of perfect knowledge in the mind
श्रूं	śrūṃ	The protection of perfect peace in the mind
स्स्रां	ssrāṃ	The consciousness of great knowledge in the perfect mind
स्स्त्रौं	sstrauṃ	The various forms of knowledge of the perfection of the divinity of tat twam asi in the mind
स्तौं	stauṃ	The perfect divine knowledge of tat twam asi
स्त्रां	strāṃ	The consciousness of the perfect knowledge of tat twam asi in the mind
स्त्रौं	strauṃ	The perfection of the divine knowledge of tat twam asi in the mind
स्त्रीं	strīṃ	The perfection of the knowledge of tat twam asi in the subtle and causal bodies

स्त्रूं	strūṃ	The protection of the perfection of tat twam asi in the mind
स्तूं	stūṃ	The protection of the perfect knowledge of tat twam asi
सूं	sūṃ	The protection of the perfect knowledge
श्व्रं	śvraṃ	The perfection of peaceful vibrations in the mind
तां	tāṃ	The perfect consciousness of tat twam asi
ठां	ṭhāṃ	The consciousness of the perfect supremacy of the great teacher
थ्लीं	thlīṃ	The protection of the perfect prayer in the gross and causal bodies
थ्प्रीं	thprīṃ	The perfect purity of prayer in the subtle and causal bodies
तीं	tīṃ	The perfection of tat twam asi in the causal body
त्रैं	traiṃ	The perfect wisdom of tat twam asi in the mind
त्रां	trāṃ	The consciousness of the perfection of tat twam asi in the mind
त्रौं	trauṃ	The divinity of the perfection of tat twam asi in the mind
त्रें	treṃ	The vibrations of the perfection of tat twam asi in the mind
त्रीं	trīṃ	The manifestation of the perfection of tat twam asi in the mind and heart
त्रों	troṃ	The manifestation of the perfection of tat twam asi in the subtle body
त्रूं	trūṃ	The protection of the perfection of tat twam asi in the mind
त्स्रां	tsrāṃ	The perfect consciousness of the knowledge of tat twam asi in the mind
त्स्रों	tsroṃ	The perfection of that divine knowledge of tat twam asi in the subtle body
ऊं	ūṃ	The perfect protection
वैं	vaiṃ	The vibrations of perfect wisdom
वं	vaṃ	The perfection of all vibrations
वां	vāṃ	The consciousness of the perfection of vibrations
वौं	vauṃ	The perfection of divine vibrations

विं	viṃ	The vibrations of perfect knowledge
वीं	vīṃ	The perfection of vibrations in the causal body
व्लीं	vlīṃ	The perfection of the vibrations of manifested existence in the causal body
व्लूं	vlūṃ	The protection of the perfect vibrations of manifested existence
व्रां	vrāṃ	The perfect consciousness of vibrations in the mind
व्रें	vreṃ	The perfect vibrations of wisdom in the mind
व्रीं	vrīṃ	The perfection of vibrations in the mind and heart
व्रीं	vrīṃ	The perfection of vibrations in the mind and in the heart
व्रूं	vrūṃ	The protection of perfect vibrations in the mind
व्यं	vyaṃ	The perfect control of vibrations
यैं	yaiṃ	The perfect control with wisdom
यं	yaṃ	The perfection of control
यां	yāṃ	The consciousness of perfect control
युं	yuṃ	The control of all circumstances for the ultimate perfection
यूं	yūṃ	The protection of the perfect control

Milton Keynes UK
Ingram Content Group UK Ltd.
UKHW010635240424
441619UK00001BA/72

9 781877 795183